THE
ILLUSTRATED HISTORY OF WEAPONS
SWORDS
SPEARS & MACES

KINGSFORDEDITIONS

Distributed by Kingsford Editions
45–55 Fairchild Street
Heatherton Victoria 3202 Australia
www.hinkler.com.au

Copyright © Hinkler Books Pty Ltd 2014

Created by Moseley Road Inc.
President: Sean Moore
Project art and editorial director: Tina Vaughan and Damien Moore
Cover design: Hinkler Design Studio
Internal design: Mark Johnson-Davies,
Andy Crisp, Kate Stretton, Philippa Baile
Photographer: Jonathan Conklin Photography, Inc.
f-stop fitzgerald
Author: David Soud
Prepress: Graphic Print Group

ISBN: 978 1 7436 3058 7

Printed and bound in China

THE
ILLUSTRATED HISTORY OF WEAPONS
SWORDS
SPEARS & MACES

David Soud

KINGSFORDEDITIONS

Contents

Introduction:
The Way of the Sword

Of all human weapons, the sword is the most charged with meaning. Though long outmoded on the battlefield, it remains the foremost symbol of war. The reason is simple enough: from the earliest stone blades through the cut and thrust of medieval and Renaissance warfare to the last cavalry charges of the modern world, the sword has been the premier instrument of close combat. Missile weapons kill at a distance; daggers are tainted by their association with criminal violence. Swords have been the trusted weapons of untold generations of warriors who have had to master their fear and confront their opponents face to face. For cultures across time and across the globe, how one conducts oneself with sword in hand is the supreme measure of character.

To say this is not to mitigate the inhumanity and often senseless savagery of war. But what is perhaps most compelling about the symbolic force of the sword is the way in which it has so often been used in opposition to those very evils. In Japan, for instance, the samurai sword, once the privileged weapon of an often brutal warrior class entrusted with enforcing a feudal order, became over time the heart of a spiritualized discipline of combat designed to teach humility and even self-transcendence. The same is true of swords in other traditions—but seldom of other weapons. The intimacy between a sword and its wielder, which has something to do with the weapon's feel in the hand, its demands on body and mind, and even its beauty as a work of art and craft, lends a fine blade to this sort of transfigured use.

This book traces the history of the sword, and of some weapons closely associated with it, from the earliest evidence of their use through the final and

SABRE HILT
The modern sword: a 19th-century sword hilt from India.

ANCIENT INDIAN SWORD
The archaic sword: a bronze blade over 3,000 years old, unearthed in India.

largely symbolic purposes to which they have been put in more recent times. Above all, it treats these weapons as cultural artifacts and works of art. Of course, no such book can be anywhere near exhaustive, but in these pages you will be able to tour the immense depth and variety of swordmaking traditions, and the values they represent.

The history of swordmaking is the story of how technical necessity, aesthetic appreciation, class consciousness, and codes of conduct intersected in the production of weapons.

On the technical side, bladesmiths continually sought new and better ways to achieve a convergence of three material qualities: rigidity, resilience, and cutting or penetrating power. It was this quest that led to crucial advances in the production of bronze, iron, and steel, some of which have actually been lost. At the

same time, a finished sword had to be ergonomically sound: balanced, maneuverable, and above all designed for the needs of its wielder in combat. The blade of a mounted warrior generally requires a very different blade geometry than the sword of a foot soldier, and someone facing enemies in heavy plate armor will likely prefer a blade made more for precise thrusts than slashing strokes.

KNIGHTS OF MALTA

The sword as object of veneration: a 17th-century cruciform sword of the Knights of Malta.

KNIGHTS IN COMBAT

A 15th-century illustration of armored knights in combat, probably in a tournament.

At the same time, a sword should convey a sense of its value by being beautiful as well as deadly. A fine blade, brilliantly polished, can itself be a thing of beauty; if a finished sword is adorned with decorative work, the effect is naturally heightened. And if that decoration can prove inspiring to the sword's wielder or disheartening to his foes, so much the better.

As soon as a sword becomes an aesthetic object—especially in societies with a warrior class of one sort or another—it also becomes a badge of status. The more rare its materials or masterful its craftsmanship, the more it establishes its owner as possessed of extraordinary resources or exceptional taste. In societies where the sword has become more symbol than actual instrument of war, its status within the social order becomes more abstract; ultimately, it may become no more than a fashion accessory.

But the sword almost never loses its association with the codes of conduct that tend to prevail, at least in theory, among soldiers who must kill their foes at close range, and who may belong to a class that prides itself on discipline and honor. It is for this reason that swords remain part of the uniform for so many armed services around the world. For all the violence inflicted with it over the millennia, the sword will surely always be a symbol of tradition, of distinction, and of duty.

All these qualities will be evident, in varying degrees, in the weapons displayed in this book. As you explore these pages, consider not only the beauty and effectiveness of the weapons you encounter, but also their symbolic value as material expressions of martial traditions, and even of the values underpinning entire civilizations. Enjoy the journey.

DRESS SWORD
The sword as fashion accessory: a 19th-century European dress sword.

LONG CHINESE SWORD
A scholar's sword with a blade of just over 31 inches, fitted with beautifully made cloisonné enamel mountings. Note how the tip of the sword is slightly rounded rather than acute.

CHINESE YANYUE

A *yanyue*, or "crescent moon," pole arm from the 19th century. Somewhat like the Japanese *naginata*, this weapon is essentially a broad, single-edged sabre blade affixed to a pole for greater reach and momentum.

19TH-CENTURY TIBETAN RITUAL SWORD

A beautiful Tibetan ceremonial sword, with a carved jade hilt and a scabbard ornamented with Tibetan letters and a lotus image.

FRENCH SABRE HILT C.1770

A classic Islamic-style French sabre hilt from about 1770. The style of the hilt, which unites Islamic and Western elements, suits the blade, which, as its decoration reveals, is in fact Turkish.

TWO SABRE HILTS

Two European sabres from the early 19th century. The one below has an unadorned "stirrup" hilt, with a single squared knuckle guard resembling a stirrup. The one above is far more ornate, with a swept three-bar hilt and an Islamic blade of Damascus steel.

BRITISH PRESENTATION SWORD

The sword as pure symbol: a British presentation sword from the 19th century.

A World without Steel

The origins of the bladed weapon rest far back in human history. Whether for self-defense, hunting, combat, or ritual use, the peoples of the Paleolithic era surely turned their capacity for tool-making to the production of weapons. The first to appear were axes and daggers; only later did the blades lengthen enough to become the first known swords. But we should not underestimate the skill and ingenuity that gave rise to these early blades. Indeed, many of the most important innovations in sword-making occurred before the classical era.

PALEOLITHIC STONE HAND-AXE
A Paleolithic hand-axe discovered in England. Though very ancient, it displays solid craftsmanship and is formed to fit neatly in the hand. Such implements were more effective than they might seem to a 21st-century reader.

JADEITE AXE
A finely polished Neolithic axe-head unearthed near Canterbury, England. Jadeite's density made it a very different sort of material to work with than easily knapped stone.

THE FIRST HARDENING TECHNIQUE

We are accustomed to thinking of Stone Age people knapping flint without any special preparation; the process seems straightforward enough, if difficult. But evidence suggests that as far back as 75,000 years ago and earlier, toolmakers were heating stones to improve their quality as tools. In what is now South Africa, toolmakers heated stones of silcrete, a mineral made of quartz grains and silica, to improve its flaking properties. The heat treatment created more crystallization in the rock, allowing it to flake in more consistent, controllable ways, and create sharper edges. The trade-off: more brittleness. The technique involved not striking stone against stone but applying carefully modulated pressure to a heated rock. It involved considerable skill. One might say that these early stoneworkers were the world's first bladesmiths.

Blades of Stone

The first blades we know of were made of stone. As tool-making gained sophistication, certain types of stone became preferred: flint, obsidian, and other kinds of rock that could take a particular kind of edge. The process of pressure flaking—also, rather loosely, known as flint-knapping—involved the skillful application of pressure with the right materials, at the right angles, to flake off bits of stone in a manner that would form precise, even razor-sharp edges. Some Paleolithic hand-axes show impressive workmanship; later Neolithic blades are genuine works of art, with expertly knapped edges and forms as beautiful as they are effective. In some cultures, such as that of the Aztecs, obsidian blades remained important ritual objects.

AZTEC WARRIORS

An image from the Florentine Codex, a 16th-century study by a Spanish Franciscan Friar, depicting Aztec warriors dressed as predators, each brandishing an obsidian-bladed weapon called a macuahuitl.

STONE KNIFE

A Neolithic stone knife excavated in France. While the technology involved is unsophisticated, the ergonomics of this tool are very good; it would nestle in the hand comfortably and be useful for a range of cutting strokes.

NEOLITHIC AXE

A Neolithic axe consisting of a wooden handle, a stone blade, and a mounting made of deer antler. It dates from about 3600 BCE.

From Stone to Bronze

While stone blades were actually very effective as both tools and weapons, they suffered from one serious drawback: they didn't last. The same pressures that, highly controlled, flaked away stone to create razor-sharp edges would, if not controlled, simply break the blade—and a broken stone blade could not be restored. It was likely the search for a more durable weapons material that led early smiths to the use of copper and then copper alloys, most importantly bronze. These metals not only held sharp edges; they could easily be resharpened—and, more importantly, they could also be repaired even when substantially damaged. Significantly, they also allowed for a greater range of forms and decoration—a benefit that craftsmen were not slow to expoit.

However, early copper and bronze weapons suffered from a fundamental structural problem common to stone weapons: finding a secure, durable way to attach the blade to hilt. In many early metal weapons, the base of the blade is tanged, and the hilt riveted to the tang. That joint proved a vulnerable point, and over time bladesmiths developed the skill to forge weapons in which the blade and hilt were cast as one piece. Most of these weapons do not really qualify as swords: they are really daggers and dirks, used for close combat when such long-distance weapons as spears and arrows were no longer in play. Gradually, however, the so-called "grip-tongue" construction of swords spread from Europe to the Middle East, and became the preferred method of forging swords.

BRONZE DAGGER FROM LURISTAN

A well-preserved Bronze Age double-edged dagger from Luristan in northwestern Iran. Cast in one piece of bronze, this sturdy weapon even has finger grooves for a sure grip. Many of the weapons found in Luristan appear to have been Babylonian in manufacture; their presence so far from their place of origin indicates how weapons technology spread quickly throughout large regions.

CURVED BRONZE AGE SWORD FROM DENMARK

A curved, broad bronze sword, c. 1600 BCE, unearthed in Denmark. The curled tip of the blade recalls similar designs in Hittite swords from what is now Turkey.

BRONZE ANTENNA SWORD HILTS

Two elegantly designed sword hilts from the late Bronze Age Halstatt culture of Central Europe. The curling pommel designs led to these weapons being called "antenna swords."

EGYPTIAN CURVED BRONZE SWORD

An Egyptian *khopesh*, a curved bronze sword from the time of Ramses II (c.1250 BCE). The hooked blade, sharpened only on the outside of its curve, delivered sabre-like slashing blows but could also be used to hook and control opponents' shields or weapons.

BRONZE SWORD FROM PERSIA

A bronze sword from Persia, 9th–8th centuries BCE. The blade's profile taper—the way it narrows as it extends from base to tip—indicates that, though it was primarily for thrusting, it was also useful for hacking and slashing.

COPPER CEREMONIAL DAGGER

A copper ceremonial dagger of the Kwakwaka'wakw people of the American Pacific Northwest. Its hilt is made of wood, nails, bone, and twine. The stylized bear's head pommel may indicate the Kwakwaka'wakw people's mythical ancestors, who were believed to have taken the form of animals. Daggers such as this were used in rituals and given as gifts.

The Advent of Iron

It is a fairly common, and understandable, misconception that iron was never used as a material during the Bronze Age. In fact, iron objects of various kinds were being made well before what we customarily call the Iron Age. And iron is in fact a much more common and accessible element than copper or tin. But somewhere around 1000 BCE, ironworking became more widespread, likely because smiths had mastered the process of extracting iron from ore with minimal impurities. By about 700 BCE it was the preferred metal for making edged weapons. Bronze is more easily worked, so it remained the material of choice for highly decorated swords, but iron is stronger and holds an edge better, so for the straightforward combat weapon it was clearly superior. In the later Iron Age, swordsmiths discovered the process of adding carbon to iron, and the steel blade was born.

No civilization was more responsible for these refinements than the La Tène culture, whose influence spread from Central Europe as far as what is now Poland, the British Isles, and the Mediterranean. The swords of the La Tène culture, mostly iron and later steel, exhibit exceptional workmanship, and their scabbards were often richly decorated. Here we see the sword not only as a weapon, but also as a badge of elite warrior status. La Tène blacksmiths also introduced such innovative techniques as pattern–welding— forging a blade from different metal rods twisted together, resulting not only in exceptionally fine edge-holding and resilience, but also in organic patterns that play across the surface of the polished blade.

IRON AGE SWORD

An early Iron Age sword with a long blade designed for thrusting. The hilt, made of bronze, is far better preserved than the heavily corroded iron blade.

IRON AGE SWORD HILT

An ornate sword hilt from the La Tène culture, c. 300 BCE. The lobed pommel and iron grip are decorated with red glass.

LA TÈNE SCABBARD

The simply but gracefully carved scabbard of a La Tène sword from c. 200 BCE. Note the stylized antelope at the top.

IRON AGE SWORD AND SPEARHEAD

An Iron Age sword and spearhead unearthed in Switzerland. They date from approximately 300 BCE.

FALCATA

A *falcata*, so named in the 19th century. These famous Iron Age swords were used by Iberian peoples well into the Roman era. Usually single-edged, their curved blades were designed to fall on opponents with the force of an axe. They were also exceptionally strong; according to records, the finest *falcatas* were made from laminated steel plates that had first been buried for two or three years so that the weaker metal would corrode away.

Classical Weapons

Greeks and Romans at War

The great civilizations of ancient Greece and Rome both adopted systematic approaches to warfare. In the Greek phalanx or the Roman legion, soldiers were trained to fight in formation and execute a range of disciplined maneuvers. In ancient Greece especially, the spear remained the most important weapon, but both Greek and Roman warriors had to be skillful with the sword.

AN IMAGE from a 5th-century BCE Attic amphora of hoplites in combat. Note that, though they wear short swords, their primary weapon is a thrusting spear.

The Classical Spear

From the battles of Homer's *Iliad* through the conquests of Alexander the Great, the spear was the linchpin of military tactics. While the thrown javelin played key roles in warfare in different periods, a long, thrusting hand-held spear was the customary weapon of Greek and Hellenistic warfare. By about 700 BCE, hoplites—the heavy infantry of Greek phalanxes—were carrying the famous *dory*, a thrusting spear some ten feet long, with a spiked butt end that could serve as a secondary weapon, especially if the shaft of the *dory* broke. Swords were used only in close combat, if formations were dispersed, either as a deliberate tactic or by the enemy.

In the 4th century BCE, Philip of Macedon brought all of Greece to heel by training his phalanxes in the coordinated use of the *sarissa*, a two-handed thrusting spear some 18 feet long. Philip's son Alexander the Great would use the *sarissa* to conquer his vast empire, and it would remain a prominent weapon in the Eastern Mediterranean well into the Byzantine era.

The Roman legions brought a different kind of industrial ingenuity to the spear. For much of the late Republic and early Empire, each legionary carried at least one throwing spear known as a *pilum*. The *pilum* was, in effect, a disposable weapon with a relatively soft iron shank with a pyramidal tip. Its role was to penetrate enemy shields or armor and, if not wound or kill an enemy warrior, at least force him to drop a shield or piece of armor. On impact, the shank would usually bend, making it impossible to turn on the Romans with their own spears. Once combat drew close, legionaries would use the *gladius*, the famous short sword of Rome.

GREEK SPEAR PARTS

A bronze Greek spearhead from about the 7th century BCE, below which are three bronze butt ends of thrusting spears, or dories. Note how some are crudely inscribed.

THE KEMPTEN PILUM

The Kempten Pilum, a Roman spearhead unearthed in England. The *pilum* was about six feet long with a pyramidal tip. Its soft iron shank almost surely bent on impact—precisely what the *pilum* was designed to do.

AMPHORA WITH HOPLITES

An ancient amphora depicting phalanxes in battle wielding dories. Though the hoplites here are all thrusting overhand, this may be an aesthetic choice; it seems that underhand thrusts and other moves also figured in *dory* combat.

CHALCIDIAN HELMET

A Chalcidian-type helmet from about 500 BCE. The cheek guards are attached by pins. Originally, the helmet would have contained a custom-fitted leather lining.

The Hoplite Sword

In the hands of the ancient Greeks, the grip–tongue swords of the late Bronze and early Iron Ages evolved into one of the most successful sword designs of the ancient world: the hoplite sword, or *xiphos*. Though *xiphos* seems to have originally referred to any kind of sword, it came to be identified with a particular form of blade. The *xiphos* was a short sword, only about two feet long and usually hung from a baldric on a warrior's left side for quick unsheathing with the right hand. Its blade was typically leaf–shaped, expanding to its widest at about two–thirds of its length and then tapering to an aggressive point; this made it useful for both cutting and thrusting. But for a hoplite, drawing a sword in the heat of battle usually meant disaster, in that the stout phalanx formation had likely been broken and his spear was of no more use to him. The *xiphos* spread alongside the rest of Greek culture: swords of a similar shape have been unearthed from North Africa through what is now Iran and into the Indian subcontinent. Even *saif*, the Arabic word for sword, is thought to have been derived from the Greek *xiphos*. The hoplite sword remains an archetypal weapon.

SCULPTURE OF HOPLITE

A 5th–century BCE Spartan sculpture of a hoplite. It presents the definitive image of a classical Greek warrior.

EARLY BRONZE SWORD

A bronze Greek short sword from before 1000 BCE. It has a curved pommel and rivets for material to aid grip, but its stout blade anticipates the advances of the later *xiphos*, with its more dramatic profile taper.

Leaf–shape blade

BRONZE XIPHOS

A well-preserved 5th–4th-century BCE bronze *xiphos* from the British Museum. With its grip–tongue construction and leaf–shaped blade, it was a balanced, versatile weapon for close combat.

THE GREEK SWORD RECONSTRUCTED

A Mycenaean sword from around 1000 BCE, together with two modern reproductions of Mycenaean swords from the National Archaeological Museum in Athens. These early swords have more acute stabbing blades than the later *xiphos*.

URN WITH ILLUSTRATION OF ACTAEON

An ancient urn depicting the violent death of Actaeon, who in this rendering attempts to defend himself with a classic *xiphos*. In Greek mythology, Actaeon was a great hunter, but he met his doom when the goddess Artemis, virginal huntress of Olympus, condemned him to be torn to pieces by his own hounds. As is often the case with myths, the story varies, but the most celebrated version relates that Actaeon stumbled upon Artemis bathing, and she was so outraged at being seen nude by a mortal that she commanded him to remain forever silent rather than speak of what he had seen. When Actaeon unconsciously responded with a cry to the calls of his hunting party, he was transformed into a stag, and his own hounds, not recognizing their master, tore him to pieces. Note the leaf–shaped blade of the *xiphos* with which Actaeon vainly tries to fight off his hounds, even as he begins to change into a stag.

POT WITH CROUCHING GREEK WARRIOR

In this ancient depiction, a Greek soldier crouches in readiness. Though his sword does not quite conform to the classical shape of the *xiphos*, the image reveals how the blade, with its short length and capacity for thrusting, might be wielded.

The Spartan Way of War

Of all the warrior traditions of the West, none is more famous than that of Sparta, the Greek city-state whose citizens' extraordinary devotion to martial discipline and civic duty made their city's name synonymous with those qualities. The founding myth of Sparta held that its lawgiver, Lycurgus, had the city walls torn down, vowing that the men of Sparta would form the only wall the city would or should ever need. This meant that the warriors of Sparta would have to be the finest in Greece—and they were.

SPARTAN HELMET
The classic bronze helmet of a Spartan warrior. It offered protection from the back of the neck to the nose and cheeks without seriously hampering peripheral vision.

IMAGE OF PHALANX
Historians produced this representation of a Greek phalanx advancing into battle. Disciplined movement and steadiness in combat were essential in this tight formation.

THE STATUE OF LEONIDAS AT THERMOPYLAE.
In this monumental sculpture, the Spartan king Leonidas wields a short sword very like a *xiphos*.

PANKRATION
An urn illustration showing two men engaged in Pankration, a martial art introduced in the ancient Greek Olympics and practiced by the warriors of Sparta. The only prohibited actions in Pankration were using weapons, biting and eye-gouging; otherwise, competitors could do whatever might bring them victory.

SPARTAN HELMET AND ARMOR

A modern but faithful reproduction of the helmet and breastplate Spartan warriors might have worn into battle. A hoplite might also have worn greaves, protective armor for the shins and sometimes the top of the foot.

HOPLITE IN COMBAT

A 5th-century BCE depiction of a hoplite wielding a spear amidst a volley of arrows. He also carries a short sword, most likely a *xiphos*, slung from a baldric.

MONUMENT TO THE BATTLE OF THERMOPYLAE

A relief commemorating the storied Battle of Thermopylae in 480 BCE. It memorializes the close, cohesive fighting style of the Greek warriors who died there—especially those who remained with King Leonidas as the doomed rear guard.

Other Ancient Greek Blades

Though the *xiphos* remains the iconic sword of ancient Greece, it was by no means the only type of blade used by Greek warriors. From around 500 BCE, the double-edged *xiphos* was supplemented by a single-edged sword with a blade curved slightly inward, called a *kopis*. It is unclear how this type of sword entered the Greek armory, but it seems most likely that it was imported from Italy or Central Europe, perhaps through the Etruscans. It seems also to have been related to the Iberian *falcata*. Made for hacking and chopping, the *kopis* was clearly not meant for phalanx warfare; the

historian Xenophon, himself a soldier and mercenary, recommended that it be used from horseback.

Another kind of sword, the *makhaira*, was similar to the *kopis*. Though the word *makhaira* was used rather broadly in ancient sources, modern scholars distinguish between the two by the profile of their blade: whereas the blade of the *kopis* curved inward, that of the *makhaira* curved slightly outward, like a sabre. It was clearly a slashing sword, suitable for use on horseback or in open rather than formation combat.

HOPLITE SINGLE COMBAT

Two hoplites engaged in one-on-one combat of the sort chronicled in Homer's Iliad. Both are armed with thrusting spears. The illustration shows the key role played by shields in ancient Greek combat.

URN ILLUSTRATION OF SOLDIER WITH MAKHAIRA

On this 5th-century BCE urn, a soldier wielding a *makhaira* falls victim to an opponent's spear thrust. The image reflects the general preference for spear over sword in ancient Greek combat.

MODERN REPLICA OF A MAKHAIRA

A modern replica of a *makhaira* from the National Archeological Museum in Athens. Its blade profile, almost lozenge-shaped but with one edge curving to a long point, indicates that it was primarily used for slashing but could manage thrusting strikes as well.

Simple ring-shaped pommel, aligned with the grip and blade

THE SWORD OF ALEXANDER

Perhaps the most famous depiction of Alexander the Great is the mosaic in Pompeii of the Battle of Issus. In the 1st–century CE mosaic, shown here, which may be a copy of a much earlier painting, Alexander rides magnificently into battle on his horse Bucephalus, wearing a medusa–badged breastplate and what appears to be a classic *xiphos* slung across his hip. However, other accounts of Alexander describe him as wielding a *makhaira*, the better to fight with on horseback. Regardless, the mosaic exemplifies the status of the *xiphos* as the standard short sword of the Hellenic and Hellenistic eras.

The Sword of Rome

In 390 BCE, an army of Celts descended from Central Europe into Italy, decimating the army of the Latin League and sacking Rome. It was a pivotal event in the history of warfare, for the simple reason that it put an end to the Greek-inspired tactics of spear-based warfare that had dominated the region for centuries. The Celts had superior iron and steel swords, and their mass charges overran the spear formations of the Latins.

By 150 BCE, the new Roman combat system of throwing spear (*pilum*), short sword (*gladius*), and heavy curved shield (*scutum*) had established Rome as the most feared military power in the Mediterranean. Those arms, and the legionaries who bore them, would build the Roman Empire.

We cannot be sure where the design of the *gladius* came from; the historian Polybius suggests that it originated in Celtic Spain. In its earliest form, the sword resembled Celtic weapons of the time; it was built mainly for thrusting rather than slashing, so as to pierce armor. As the empire expanded and legions encountered peoples who wore little armor and preferred a less disciplined form of combat, the *gladius* blade was shortened and broadened to allow for more hacking and slashing.

Eventually, around the 2nd century CE, the old system of *scutum* and *gladius* was deemed obsolete, and a new sword, the *spatha*, was introduced. Originally a cavalry sword, the *spatha* had a blade about two feet long and a short point—it was built for slashing, not thrusting. Eventually, as the Germanic tribes absorbed the influence of Roman tactics, Roman and Germanic swords became virtually indistinguishable.

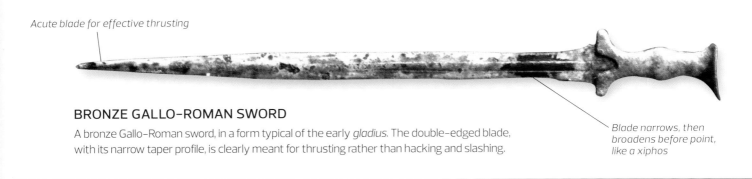

Acute blade for effective thrusting

Blade narrows, then broadens before point, like a xiphos

BRONZE GALLO-ROMAN SWORD

A bronze Gallo-Roman sword, in a form typical of the early *gladius*. The double-edged blade, with its narrow taper profile, is clearly meant for thrusting rather than hacking and slashing.

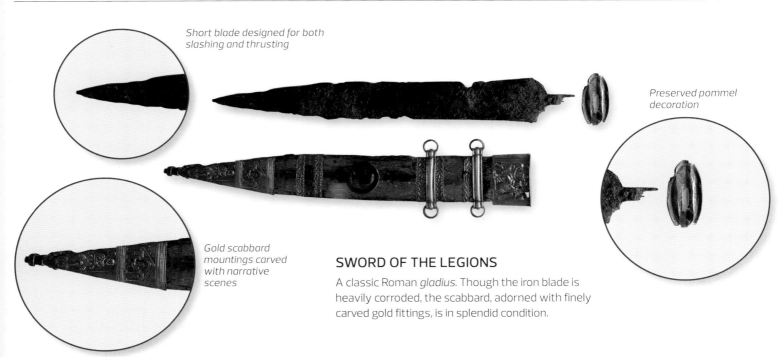

Short blade designed for both slashing and thrusting

Preserved pommel decoration

Gold scabbard mountings carved with narrative scenes

SWORD OF THE LEGIONS

A classic Roman *gladius*. Though the iron blade is heavily corroded, the scabbard, adorned with finely carved gold fittings, is in splendid condition.

ROMAN GRAVESTONE

The gravestone of Quintus Petilius Secundus, a legionary who died in the 1st century CE. He is depicted armed with a *pilum*, a dagger, and a classic *gladius*, which is worn on his right hip as was customary.

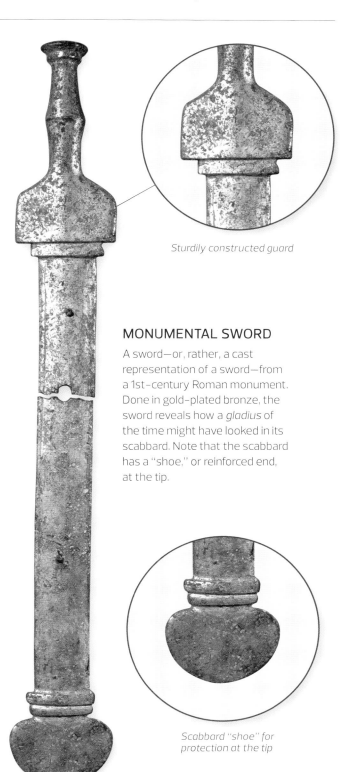

Sturdily constructed guard

MONUMENTAL SWORD

A sword—or, rather, a cast representation of a sword—from a 1st-century Roman monument. Done in gold–plated bronze, the sword reveals how a *gladius* of the time might have looked in its scabbard. Note that the scabbard has a "shoe," or reinforced end, at the tip.

Scabbard "shoe" for protection at the tip

Medieval Weapons

The Cut and Thrust of Medieval Weapons

After the decline and fall of the Roman Empire, much of its order gave way to migrations, conflicts, and disarray. But these were hardly the "Dark Ages" that Renaissance thinkers first characterized them to be; much of the old order was absorbed into the new, and among the traditions to endure were those of weaponry. The Roman *spatha* evolved into the legendary swords of the Anglo–Saxons, the Vikings, and even the knights of the Crusades. And, as armor became more sophisticated and effective, new roles were found for such primal weapons as the mace and the flail.

MOUNTED KNIGHTS in combat from a 14th-century manuscript.

Germanic Swords

The Celts had established the finest swordmaking tradition in Europe well before the decline of the Roman Empire, and it was from the merging of Northern forging techniques and Roman blade profiles that the Germanic sword first arose. In Germanic culture, the sword was the supreme weapon, and fine blades were handed down as heirlooms and given ceremonially as gifts.

Though single-bladed swords such as the *seax* were common in the 5th through 7th centuries, the classic Germanic sword is a double-edged, straight-bladed weapon that occupies a middling position between the Roman *spatha* and the cut-and-thrust sword of the later Middle Ages. Their blades were of iron or steel, sometimes pattern-welded, and their mountings could be astounding works of art.

Long tang for balance and solidity between hilt and blade

VIKING SEAX

The Seax of Beagnoth, found in England, and titled after the name—perhaps the owner's—inscribed in Viking runes along the spine of the blade. The single-edged blade is about 22 inches long.

Viking runes along the spine of the blade

REPRODUCTION OF LOMBARD SWORD

A modern reproduction of a 6th-century Lombard sword. Clearly modeled on the Roman *spatha*, this blade was made for slashing.

Sturdy crossguard for the rigors of combat

Substantial, securely bolted pommel

6TH-CENTURY SWORD HILT

A 6th-century CE Anglo-Saxon hilt unearthed on the Isle of Wight. The intricate, beautiful metalwork was a hallmark of fine Anglo-Saxon swords.

Intricate gold serpentine design at base of blade

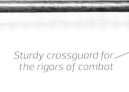

Warrior in wolf costume with sword

THE GUTENSTEIN SCABBARD

An ornate silver 7th-century Germanic scabbard. One of its images shows a warrior in a wolf costume holding a large sword.

Ornamental pommel cap

GERMANIC HILT

Though corroded with age and exposure, this Germanic hilt has been displayed in a manner that reveals how it was bolted together.

Thick, sturdy guard

Viking Swords

Vikings are among the most storied warriors and sword-wielders in all of history, not least because their own stories of war and heroic deeds are rich and fascinating documents. For centuries, the Vikings traded and raided as far as their formidable seafaring skills would take them. They reached North America centuries before Colombus, and Nordic artifacts have been found in period sites as distant as India.

No possession was more prized among the Vikings than a fine sword. Norsemen treasured their swords, treated them as prizes, heirlooms and valued signs of honor and achievement. They even gave them names. The Norse sagas are full of stories in which heroes wield great swords, and duels are fought over honor. And it was Viking warriors who famously formed the core of the elite Varangian Guard of Byzantium.

Large pommel for balance and control

EARLY VIKING SWORD

An early Viking sword from the Bergen Museum in Norway. Much like a Roman *spatha*, it has an abrupt rather than gradually tapered point, and a very substantial hilt.

VIKING SWORD WITH SILVER HILT

A classic Viking sword with a silver-inlaid hilt, 10th or 11th century. Still visible on the blade is a single wide fuller (groove) to make the blade lighter and stiffer.

Single wide fuller

8TH-CENTURY VIKING SWORD

An 8th-century Viking sword unearthed in Norway. Its long, two-edged blade has a point just acute enough to allow for thrusting, but it is much more suitable for hacking and slashing. Note how the large pommel—a hallmark of Viking swords—balances the long blade.

Gradual, not acute, profile taper to blade

DECORATED VIKING HILT

The remains of a 10th-century Viking hilt, showing traces of the elaborate serpentine motifs that characterized much Norse and Germanic decoration.

Serpentine motif

ORNATE VIKING HILT

This 9th-century Viking hilt from Scotland is exceptionally fine, with highly detailed silver inlay over classic Viking construction.

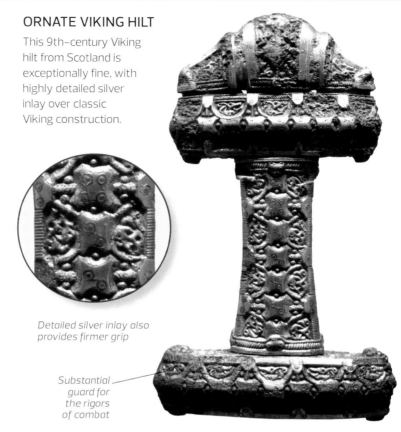

Detailed silver inlay also provides firmer grip

Substantial guard for the rigors of combat

Silver work on pommel

Corrosion on a relatively unprotected portion of the blade

Characteristic large pommel for balance

The Art and Technology of Late Viking Swords

From the 8th to the 10th centuries, Viking swords were the pinnacle of the swordsmith's art. They were superbly balanced, that effect being partly achieved through large, artfully designed pommels. Many blades were pattern-welded in sophisticated fashion, with iron and steel rods twisted together to form the center of the blade and the edges then welded on. The resulting patterns were often highlighted with acid etching. Most of the blades were also fullered (having a groove down the length of the blade to make it lighter and more agile without sacrificing strength). The pride of Viking swordsmiths and owners is evinced in the many names inlaid in the fullered groove.

9TH-CENTURY VIKING SWORD

A 9th-century Viking sword, badly corroded. It was buried in England with its owner, a warrior in his late 30s who stood about six feet tall and died in battle.

Part of the pommel missing

Substantial crossguard

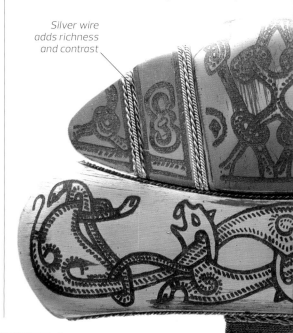

REPRODUCTION POMMEL

A careful reproduction of the decorative work on a 9th-century Viking sword. The lobed construction and serpentine decorative motifs are hallmarks of Viking workmanship.

Silver wire adds richness and contrast

Silver runes inscribed in blade

INSCRIPTION ON VIKING SWORD

An inscription of silver runes inlaid in the steel blade of a Norwegian sword. Such inscriptions usually indicate the name of the swordsmith; owner's names were more often placed on the hilt.

MAGICAL BLADES OF THE SAGAS

The Norse sagas are full of swords, and some of them are magical. Quite a few are even cursed. One such sword is Tyrfing, a gold-hilted sword that would never miss its target, never rust, and never fail to cut through any substance. But its makers, a pair of captive dwarves, curse the blade, so that it will always do evil. First, it brings about the death of its original owner, the hero Svafrlami. Only after it causes three murders does the curse lift.

As famous as Tyrfing is, the most storied of magical swords is Gram, the sword of Siegmund in the Volsung stories. After the god Odin leaves Gram stuck in a tree, only Siegmund can remove it. Later, Odin himself duels Siegmund and shatters the blade. Siegmund leaves its shards to his son Siegfried, who reforges Gram and uses it to slay the dragon Fafnir. The story provided part of the inspiration for J. R. R. Tolkien's epic novel *The Lord of the Rings*.

Heavy corrosion on blade

Riveted construction for durability in battle

Reinforced cross-bar

Iron rivets

Viking decorative motif of twined beasts

Attachment for chin strap

Face-guard

VIKING BATTLE HELMET

A Viking battle helmet with protection for the upper face. Contrary to many popular depictions, Vikings did not wear helmets with horns on them.

Ulfberht Swords

Because the Vikings prized their swords above all other possessions, the finest swordsmiths were sought out. Their blades were revered for being able to hold an edge, to combine stiffness and resilience, and to show beautiful finish work. One name reigns supreme in that sense: Ulfberht. Ulfberht swords, which were made between about 850 and 1050, are the paragons of Viking weaponry; the quality of their steel, which was obtained from Iran and Afghanistan, was unmatched in their day and for centuries after.

INSCRIBED SWORD
An exceptionally well-preserved Ulfberht sword, from the Neues Museum Berlin. The inscription stands out clearly and the large, lobed pommel is a classic Viking feature.

Exceptionally large and sturdy guard and pommel

Inscription inlaid in silver

Geometric decoration on hilt

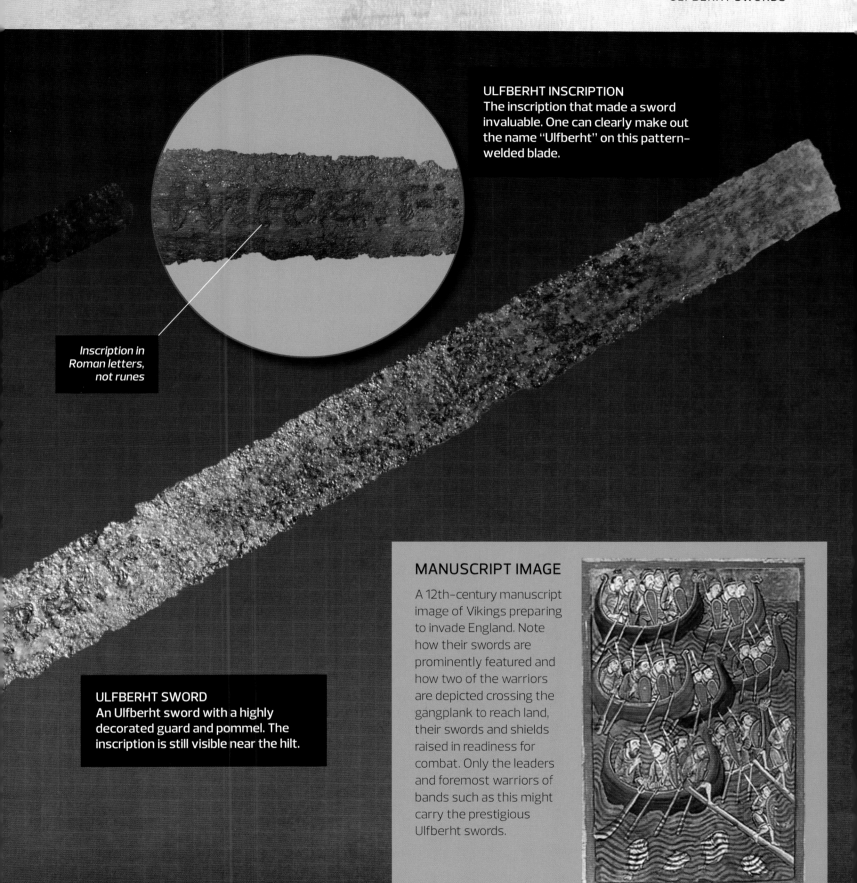

ULFBERHT INSCRIPTION
The inscription that made a sword invaluable. One can clearly make out the name "Ulfberht" on this pattern-welded blade.

Inscription in Roman letters, not runes

ULFBERHT SWORD
An Ulfberht sword with a highly decorated guard and pommel. The inscription is still visible near the hilt.

MANUSCRIPT IMAGE
A 12th-century manuscript image of Vikings preparing to invade England. Note how their swords are prominently featured and how two of the warriors are depicted crossing the gangplank to reach land, their swords and shields raised in readiness for combat. Only the leaders and foremost warriors of bands such as this might carry the prestigious Ulfberht swords.

Viking and Germanic Spears

The sword may have held pride of place among Viking and Germanic weapons, but the spear remained an vital asset. Viking spearheads were made with the same techniques that produced their magnificent swords. Many were pattern-welded and richly decorated. The spears of the Frankish Carolingians, rulers of much of Europe who reached their peak under Charlemagne (742–814), were of similar quality.

Though records and stories of the era mention spears being thrown in combat, they were much more likely to be used as thrusting weapons, for the simple reason that losing one's spear to the enemy—precisely the problem circumvented by the Roman *pilum*—could prove a deadly turn of events on the field of battle. While we cannot know how long most Viking and Carolingian spears were—period illustrations are unreliable, and the spear shafts were made of wood—they were most likely around seven feet in length, and many were designed with metal butts to balance their spearheads.

VIKING SOCKET SPEARHEAD

A Viking spearhead unearthed in England. The leaf-shaped blade is pattern-welded, and you can see where the shaft was attached to the spearhead with a socket and a small rivet.

LONG VIKING SPEARHEAD

A 9th–11th-century Viking spearhead of a particularly elegant shape. The long, tapered, triangular blade is clearly designed to pierce armor.

KOVEL SPEARHEAD

An archival image of both sides of the famous Kovel spearhead, an East Germanic spearhead found in northern Ukraine. The weapon itself was looted by the Nazis during the Second World War, and has remained lost.

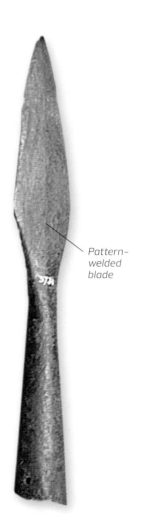

Pattern-welded blade

Triangular blade for stiffness and penetrating power

Inscription, believed to read "thither rider"

SPEARHEAD OF DAHMSDORF-MÜNCHEBERG

This spearhead was unearthed in Germany in the 19th century. Its runic inscription reads "router."

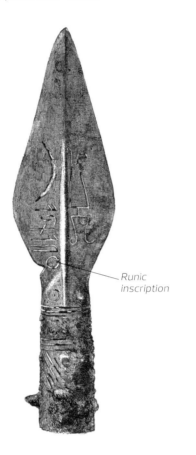

Runic inscription

GERMANIC SPEARHEAD INSCRIPTION

A North Germanic spearhead with a crude inscription, colorized in the image for easier viewing. The spear was clearly named by its owner.

CAROLINGIAN SPEARHEAD

This "winged" Carolingian spearhead from the 7th–10th centuries has a long blade reminiscent of Roman swords.

"Wing" characteristic of Merovingian and Carolingian spearheads

ODIN'S MAGIC SPEAR

In the myths and legends of the Vikings, swords were not the only magical weapons. In the *Eddas*—great epics of the North, written down in the 13th century—the leader of the gods, Odin, takes as his weapon a spear called Gungnir. Made by the great dwarf blacksmith Dvalin, who also made the cursed sword Tyrfing, Gungnir, which means "swaying one" in Old Norse, is said to have magical runes incised in its tip. It is so impeccably balanced that it never fails to strike its intended target. The mischievous god Loki managed to finagle the spear away from the dwarves as a way of atoning for one of his pranks, and it becomes the trusted weapon of Odin. At Ragnarok, the battle at the end of the world, Odin is to wield Gungnir in his climactic combat with the Fenris Wolf. In Wagner's famous operatic cycle *The Ring of the Nibelung*, based on Norse and Germanic legends, the shaft of Gungnir is made from Yggdrasil, the world tree, and Odin uses it to shatter the magic sword Gram, wielded by Siegmund. Later, Siegmund's son Siegfried breaks Gungnir.

The Medieval Battle-axe

People tend to think of axes as heavy, cumbersome things—a natural enough conclusion when most modern axes are made for splitting wood, felling trees, or doing demolition work. But the medieval battle-axe was an altogether different instrument: balanced, maneuverable, and surprisingly light.

The most famous battle-axes of medieval times were those of the Vikings, who are often depicted wielding fearsome axes, usually of a fairly short length for close combat. As archaeological evidence serves to indicate, Scandinavian and Germanic warriors often used battle-axes to cleave the legs of their opponents, below their shield and armor. Throwing-axes became popular weapons as well.

The narrow, cleaving blades of battle-axes could concentrate the force of impact on a precise area. The resulting cutting power could not only sever limbs, but also penetrate plate armor. It was this ability to match the increasingly formidable armor of the late medieval period that brought battle-axes to prominence in the 14th and 15th centuries.

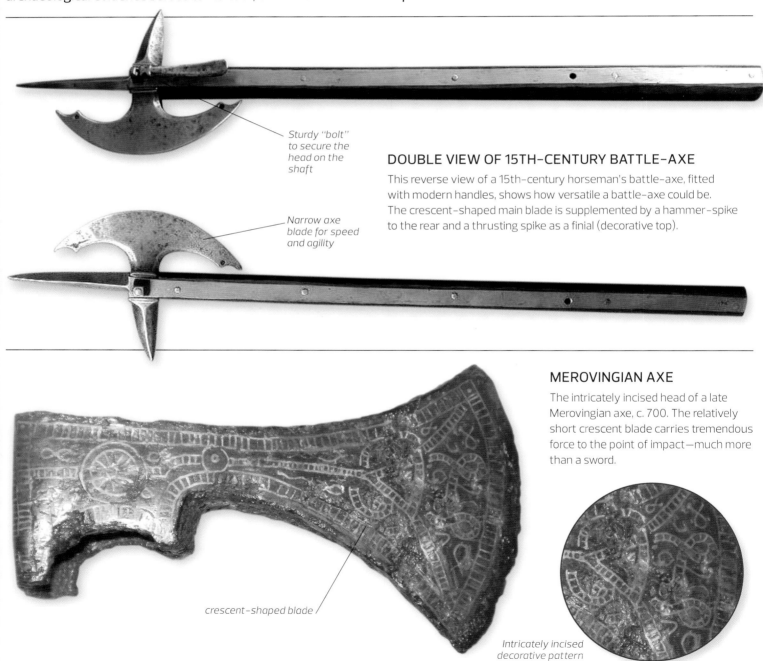

Sturdy "bolt" to secure the head on the shaft

Narrow axe blade for speed and agility

DOUBLE VIEW OF 15TH-CENTURY BATTLE-AXE

This reverse view of a 15th-century horseman's battle-axe, fitted with modern handles, shows how versatile a battle-axe could be. The crescent-shaped main blade is supplemented by a hammer-spike to the rear and a thrusting spike as a finial (decorative top).

MEROVINGIAN AXE

The intricately incised head of a late Merovingian axe, c. 700. The relatively short crescent blade carries tremendous force to the point of impact—much more than a sword.

crescent-shaped blade

Intricately incised decorative pattern

THE BLOW OF A MIGHTY AXE

In June of 1314, a large English army under the immensely unpopular King Edward II headed into Scotland to relieve besieged Stirling Castle and crush a Scottish rebellion led by Robert the Bruce, a charismatic leader and a seasoned warrior. Bruce and his captains took a position near Bannock Burn, where the more heavily armed and mounted English would be at a disadvantage. But the signal event took place before battle was joined. Henry de Bohun, an ambitious English knight in the vanguard of Edward's army, caught sight of Bruce riding alone and unarmored on a small horse some distance from his troops. Determined to seize a chance at glory, de Bohun galloped his war horse toward Bruce, his lance lowered. While soldiers on both sides watched, Bruce simply waited for de Bohun to get close, slipped the lance, and brought his battle-axe down so hard that he split de Bohun's helmet and head, killing him on the spot. The shaft of Bruce's axe broke with the force of the blow. It was a sign of things to come, as the Battle of Bannockburn would become the greatest victory of the Scots over the English.

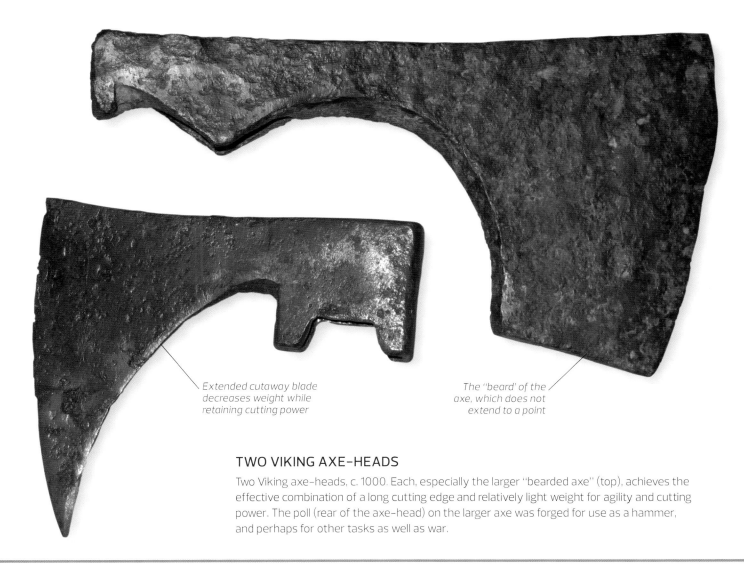

Extended cutaway blade decreases weight while retaining cutting power

The "beard" of the axe, which does not extend to a point

TWO VIKING AXE-HEADS

Two Viking axe-heads, c. 1000. Each, especially the larger "bearded axe" (top), achieves the effective combination of a long cutting edge and relatively light weight for agility and cutting power. The poll (rear of the axe-head) on the larger axe was forged for use as a hammer, and perhaps for other tasks as well as war.

From Hacking and Slashing to Cutting and Thrusting

When we think of medieval knights, we tend to envision those who fought in the Crusades, that series of military expeditions to the Holy Land that spanned the 11th through the 13th centuries. Unfortunately, very few examples of Crusader weapons have survived, and our best knowledge of them comes from manuscript illustrations and tomb effigies of the period. Though single-bladed hacking swords called falchions were also used, the typical medieval knightly sword, known as an arming sword, was designed chiefly for hacking and slashing against leather armor and chain mail but could, in a pinch, thrust as well. Its blade was usually broad at the base, with a continuous taper to an acute point.

By the end of the Crusades, swords had become longer, and more fitted to cutting and thrusting than hacking and slashing. Their blades, extending beyond three feet, were often double-fullered to shave weight and fitted with heftier pommels for balance. Blades also became narrower. This form of sword would not, however, serve well against the more advanced forms of armor developed toward the end of the Middle Ages.

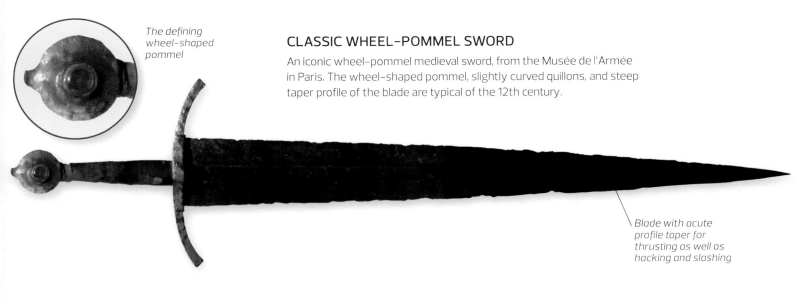

The defining wheel-shaped pommel

CLASSIC WHEEL-POMMEL SWORD

An iconic wheel-pommel medieval sword, from the Musée de l'Armée in Paris. The wheel-shaped pommel, slightly curved quillons, and steep taper profile of the blade are typical of the 12th century.

Blade with acute profile taper for thrusting as well as hacking and slashing

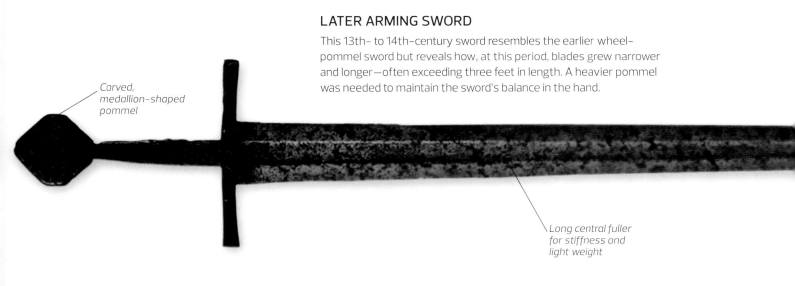

LATER ARMING SWORD

This 13th- to 14th-century sword resembles the earlier wheel-pommel sword but reveals how, at this period, blades grew narrower and longer—often exceeding three feet in length. A heavier pommel was needed to maintain the sword's balance in the hand.

Carved, medallion-shaped pommel

Long central fuller for stiffness and light weight

Richly worked gold plate on scabbard

RELIGIOUS CEREMONIAL SWORD

The Sword of Essen, given in 993 by Holy Roman Emperor Otto III to Essen Abbey in Germany, now Essen Cathedral. The workmanship of the gold-plated hilt and scabbard is exquisite.

Jewel-encrusted pommel

THE USES OF A CRUCIFORM HILT

It would be easy to think of the cruciform sword of the Middle Ages as the classic cut-and-thrust weapon, its guard meant solely to protect gauntleted hands in the fury of clashing blades. But the Medieval cruciform sword was more than a practical design; it also served as an object of devotion. With the sword turned point-downward, the hilt became a Christian cross, which could be used for prayer, meditation, or encouragement. This symbolism took on special significance during the Crusades, which were ostensibly pilgrimages with a wholly religious justification. Before battle, in meditative moments, and at funerals for fallen crusaders, the cruciform hilt became something of an icon. And it retained that significance. To "swear on one's sword" often meant to swear by the Cross. This symbolism remained powerful even in Shakespeare's day. In the first act of *Hamlet*, the prince has his companions swear upon his sword not to reveal the existence of his father's ghost; they are thus doubly sworn, both as his retainers and as Christians.

CRUCIFORM SWORD HILT

A classic cruciform sword hilt from the 14th century, with wheel pommel and straight quillons. Note the relatively narrow blade with a single fuller.

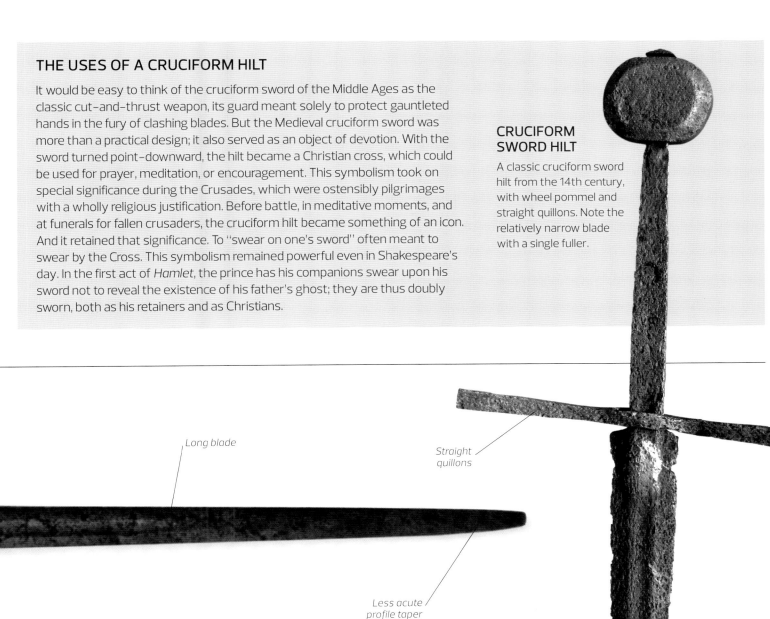

Long blade

Straight quillons

Less acute profile taper and point

The Medieval Sword Reinvented

The arrival of effective plate armor in the late 1300s, along with the increasing deadliness of such projectile weapons as the English longbow, precipitated changes in the sword. The arming sword gave way to the longsword—long in both handle and blade. The blades of the two-handed swords of the 14th through 16th centuries exceeded four and sometimes even five feet in length. To the eye, these two-handed and hand-and-a-half or "bastard" swords seem heavy and awkward, but in fact they were surprisingly light—often under seven pounds—and very well balanced. Wielding the longest blades, however, required exceptional skill. As the 14th century progressed, two-handed swords also became symbols of political as well as military power, and were often ceremonially carried before rulers and other powerful figures. Such swords are generally referred to as "bearing swords."

To counter the stoutness of plate armor, another kind of sword was also invented. Called the *estoc* or "tuck" sword, it was a thrusting weapon designed to penetrate gaps in armor with its point. *Estoc* blades were rigid and narrow, often with diamond-shaped cross sections. In the 14th century, a well-equipped knight might carry two swords: a cut-and-thrust sword and an *estoc*.

Maltese cross hilt

Slightly ovoid grip

Engravings enhance the symbolic value of the sword

Finely engraved

KNIGHTS OF MALTA SWORD

A 17th-century cruciform sword of the Knights of Malta, or Knights Hospitallers, whose original commission was to protect travelers to the Holy Land during the Crusades. With its long, widely fullered blade and "hand-and-a-half" grip for use with one or two hands, this weapon recalls the longswords of the late Medieval period.

Long blade for one- or two-handed use

SWEDISH BASTARD SWORD

A 15th-century Swedish bastard sword. The blade is long but finely tapered, and the sword well-balanced. The handle allows for both one-handed attacks and powerful two-handed cuts and thrusts.

KNIGHT'S LONGSWORD

A 15th-century knight's longsword. The substantial pommel balances the long blade physically, while the flared quillons (only one remains) added visual balance as well as hand protection.

Forward-angled crossguard (one missing)

Long blade requiring two-handed use

Forward-angled guard

THE LATE MEDIEVAL SWORD CAPTURED IN PAINT

Because relatively few medieval swords have come down in fair condition—and those that have survived tend to be similar in type—historians have had to consult manuscript illustrations, tomb effigies, and even stained-glass windows to refine their understanding of the design, wearing, and wielding of swords. Similarly, the paintings of the Renaissance often provide clues as to how late medieval swords were carried and used. One example is the c. 1500 *Paumgartner Altarpiece* by Albrecht Dürer. On his left hip, St. Eustace wears a bastard sword of the kind common among cavalrymen and mercenaries of the late Middle Ages and early Renaissance; on his right hip is a dagger. His armor is that of a mounted soldier. Paintings like this extend our vision beyond the artifact itself to its place on the battlefield, in courtly settings, and in daily life. The very angles at which Dürer's Eustace wears his swords reveals something of the practical and stylistic considerations of Northern European cavalrymen in the late 15th century.

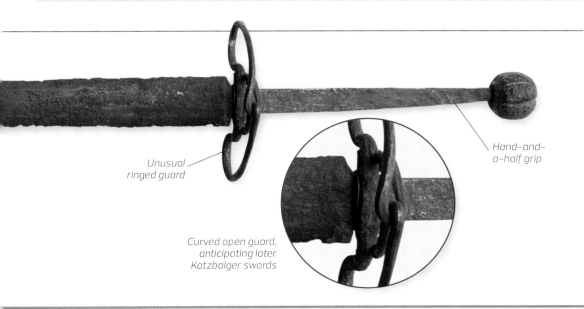

Unusual ringed guard

Curved open guard, anticipating later Katzbalger swords

Hand-and-a-half grip

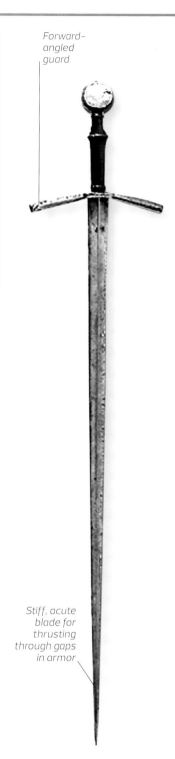

Stiff, acute blade for thrusting through gaps in armor

15TH-CENTURY ESTOC

A 15th-century Spanish *estoc*. The acute blade is designed to slip between the gaps in plate armor. Though elegant in profile, it is rigid and strong. Most *estocs* had blades about three feet long.

The Great Swords of the Late Middle Ages

The divergent evolution of the late medieval sword—simultaneously into an acute thrusting weapon and into a long, intimidating blade—prefigured developments in the Renaissance. The thrusting sword would reach its fruition in the rapier and its descendants, while the great sword would become an iconic symbol, used as a bearing sword or held by the personal bodyguards of Renaissance princes.

Even in the late Middle Ages, the two-handed great sword was a symbol. It could represent either authority or,

more commonly, extraordinary military prowess. Mercenaries and other soldiers, most famously the flamboyant Germanic *landsknechts* ("land's knights" or "land's servants") of the early Renaissance, made use of their *zweihanders*, or two-handed swords, to break up enemy pike formations or protect commanders and standard bearers. The blade of a *zweihander* could be as long as six feet—a difficult weapon to wield in close combat, but highly effective in certain situations.

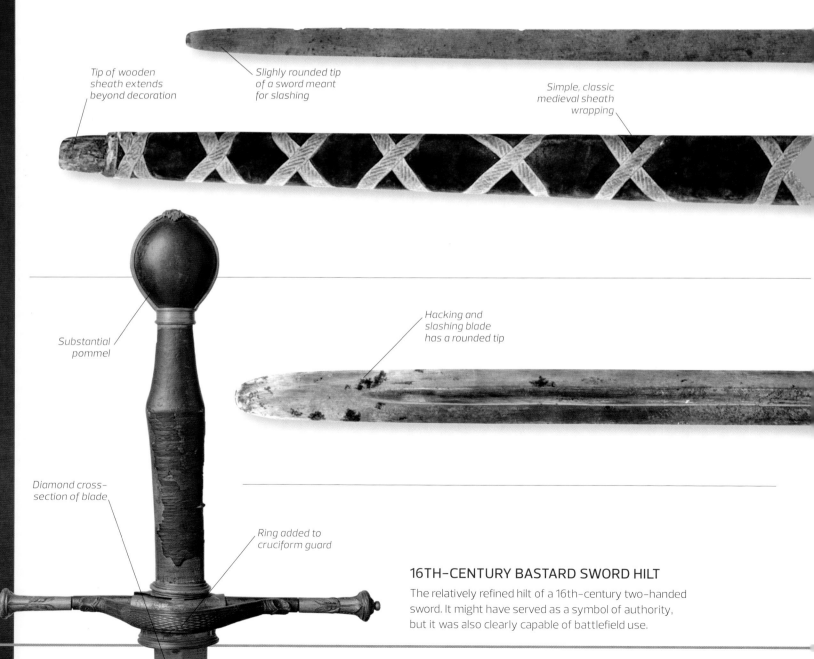

Tip of wooden sheath extends beyond decoration

Slighly rounded tip of a sword meant for slashing

Simple, classic medieval sheath wrapping

Substantial pommel

Hacking and slashing blade has a rounded tip

Diamond cross-section of blade

Ring added to cruciform guard

16TH–CENTURY BASTARD SWORD HILT

The relatively refined hilt of a 16th-century two-handed sword. It might have served as a symbol of authority, but it was also clearly capable of battlefield use.

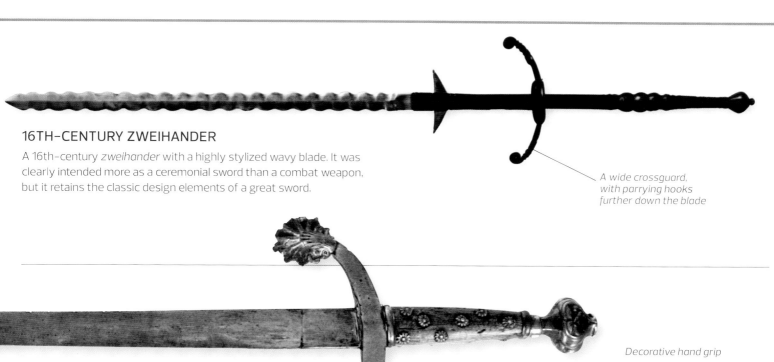

16TH-CENTURY ZWEIHANDER

A 16th-century *zweihander* with a highly stylized wavy blade. It was clearly intended more as a ceremonial sword than a combat weapon, but it retains the classic design elements of a great sword.

A wide crossguard, with parrying hooks further down the blade

Decorative hand grip

GREAT SWORD

A finely made 16th-century great sword, bearing the scars of combat but also highly ornamented, especially in its elaborately tipped quillons. The large pommel not only balanced the sword, but also helped ensure a firm grip with both hands.

Substantial pommel to balance the heavy blade

LANDSKNECHT SWORD

A formidable *landsknecht* sword from the 16th century. This weapon features a very sturdy guard and a wide central fuller to keep its weight manageable. While it could be used against enemy soldiers, it was most commonly employed to sweep aside or cut enemy pikes and break up infantry formations.

HEAVILY ARMED

What a nobleman in a late Renaissance suit of plate armor would look like carrying a bastard sword. A formidable opponent indeed.

Maces and Flails

The invention of plate armor in the 13th century led to another shift in weaponry: the increased popularity of maces and flails. Maces, which are essentially war clubs with weighted heads, are among the oldest human weapons; clubs studded with spikes of flint have been found among relics from over 10,000 years ago. Flails place the weighted striking surface at the end of a chain attached to a handle.

When first chain mail and then plate armor made cutting and slashing attacks increasingly difficult, maces became inexpensive and effective alternatives. The blow of a heavy mace can do enormous damage without having to actually penetrate armor; the force is simply transferred through the protective chains or plates to the body underneath. From the 12th century onward, maces increasingly featured flanges—raised edges of metal—that created a smaller, more concentrated point of impact and could even rupture plate

armor. While it is often claimed that bishops and other ecclesiasts used maces in war so as not to shed blood, this appears to be a myth, as there are many surviving characterizations of churchmen bearing edged weapons.

Flails are simply maces in which the head is attached to the handle by a length of chain. While requiring more skill to control than maces, flails had the added advantage of being able to "wrap around" an opponent's shield or parrying sword and inflict serious wounds. Like some maces, many flails had spiked heads for penetrating armor.

While most maces and flails were under three feet long and used by foot soldiers, horsemen occasionally used long-shafted maces. The physics of an equestrian mace—a weighted club with a long moment arm, swung at high speed by a knight already traveling extremely fast on a galloping horse—was devastating.

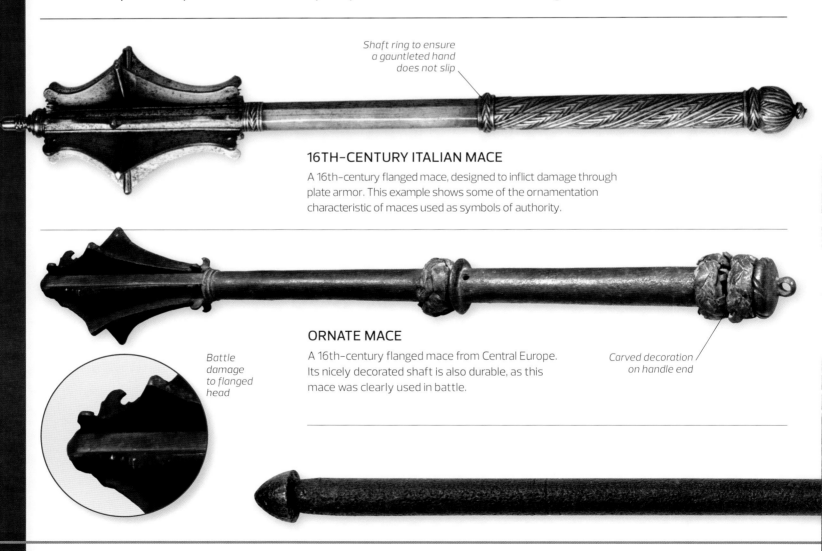

Shaft ring to ensure a gauntleted hand does not slip

16TH-CENTURY ITALIAN MACE

A 16th-century flanged mace, designed to inflict damage through plate armor. This example shows some of the ornamentation characteristic of maces used as symbols of authority.

ORNATE MACE

A 16th-century flanged mace from Central Europe. Its nicely decorated shaft is also durable, as this mace was clearly used in battle.

Battle damage to flanged head

Carved decoration on handle end

Spikes have considerable penetrating power

Wooden shaft

MORGENSTERN

A 16th-century morgenstern, or morning star, named for the spikes radiating from its head. This wooden-shafted mace was clearly not a commander's weapon: it is all about its deadly function in combat.

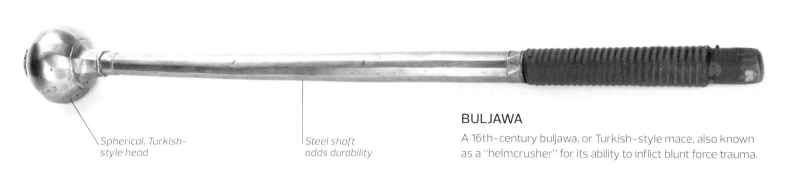

Spherical, Turkish-style head

Steel shaft adds durability

BULJAWA

A 16th-century buljawa, or Turkish-style mace, also known as a "helmcrusher" for its ability to inflict blunt force trauma.

ODO ON THE BAYEUX TAPESTRY

Bishop Odo of Bayeux as depicted on the Bayeux Tapestry, which he may have commissioned. The image shows Odo, half-brother of William the Conqueror, wielding a mace as he urges on Norman troops at the Battle of Hastings.

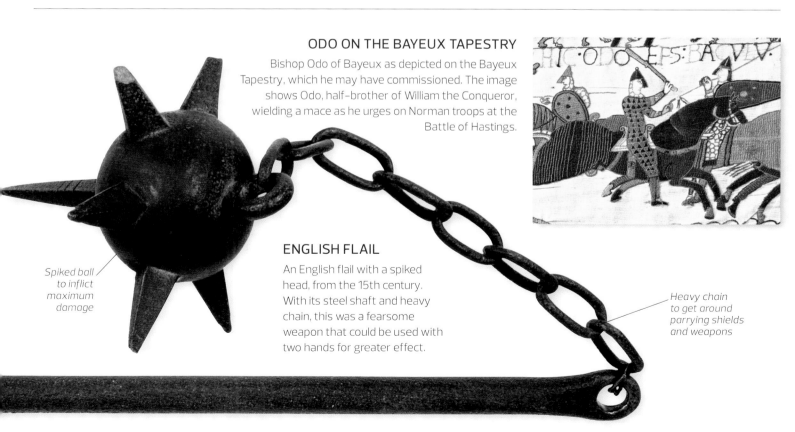

Spiked ball to inflict maximum damage

ENGLISH FLAIL

An English flail with a spiked head, from the 15th century. With its steel shaft and heavy chain, this was a fearsome weapon that could be used with two hands for greater effect.

Heavy chain to get around parrying shields and weapons

Renaissance Weapons

Renaissance of Blades

As the Middle Ages gave way to the Renaissance, the sword began to give way to the gun. The cut-and-thrust blades of the late medieval period were outmoded, and swords increasingly became civilian weapons—employed as a means of self-defense and indicators of status and wealth. The elegance and artistry of swordmaking came to the fore, and hilts became more prominent features than blades. This was the age of the rapier.

RUBENS'S COPY of Leonardo da Vinci's lost painting *The Battle of Anghiari*. It depicts four soldiers struggling for control of a battle standard during the 1440 battle between forces of Milan and those of the Italian League, led by Florence.

Vestiges of the Middle Ages

The longswords, bastard swords, and two-handed swords of the late Middle Ages did not completely disappear in the Renaissance; rather, they took on new roles or modified designs. Great swords became more ornate, and were increasingly used as intimidating symbols of authority, either as bearing swords or as forceful displays of military prowess by elite guards. Late medieval swords also evolved into broadswords—heavy, cut-and-thrust blades for military use, fitted with basket hilts—as well as such varieties as the

German "cat skinner" sword, also made for cutting and thrusting. Military swords would retain these durable forms, in contrast to the more slender and nimble civilian weapons.

Perhaps the most famous version of the broadsword is the Scottish claymore. Though claymores were originally two-handed swords usually with simple cruciform hilts, their most famous incarnations were fitted with basket hilts. These swords became iconic weapons of the Highland Regiments that fought for the British Empire.

MAXIMILIAN I PALLASK

The pallask was a combat sword with a long, two-edged blade with an acute enough point to pierce the chain mail of Ottoman cavalry. This sword, presented to the Holy Roman Emperor Maximilian I, is a superb example of this style.

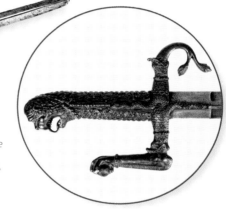

The hilt of the Maximilian I pallask, ornately formed and decorated to resemble a monster, perhaps a chimera. The pommel is the monster's head and one of the quillons is its tail. The other quillon, shaped like an arm holding a ball, forms a close knuckle guard.

Monster's head pommel

Rounded blade tip

INNSBRUCK SWORD

A finely made sword with an elaborate, almost rapier-style guard, manufactured around 1570 by the German swordsmith Ulrich Diefstetter for a member of the personal guard of Austrian Archduke Ferdinand of the Habsburg family. In a touch reminiscent of Japanese swords, the grip is made of sharkskin.

Intricate basket hilt

ITALIAN BROADSWORD

A 17th-century Italian broadsword, known as a *schiavona*. The basket hilt, similar to the intricate hilts of Renaissance rapiers, offered excellent protection for the hand, so that a gauntlet was not required.

Long hacking and slashing blade

CLAYMORE

A later version of the Scottish claymore, as worn by British Highland Scots regiments. It retains the basket hilt that characterized many earlier claymores.

The Evolution of the Civilian Sword

The most important factor in the evolution of the Renaissance sword was its new status as a civilian weapon of self-defense. This shift had two major consequences. The first was practical: a civilian sword had to be agile for ease of wielding against an unarmored foe in the sudden violence of city streets or, less commonly, country roads. The second was decorative: a sword became a fashion accessory, proclaiming its bearer's status and inviting admiration. Connoisseurship extended from a sword's strength and resilience to its workmanship and style.

Predictably, the rise in civilian swords also led to a refined culture of recreational fencing and, more problematically, dueling. Feuds like the one so memorably dramatized by Shakespeare in *Romeo and Juliet* became so problematic that in some cities statutes against dueling had to be imposed. The sword at one's waist could easily present itself as a solution to an argument, especially when one was eager to test one's skill in using it.

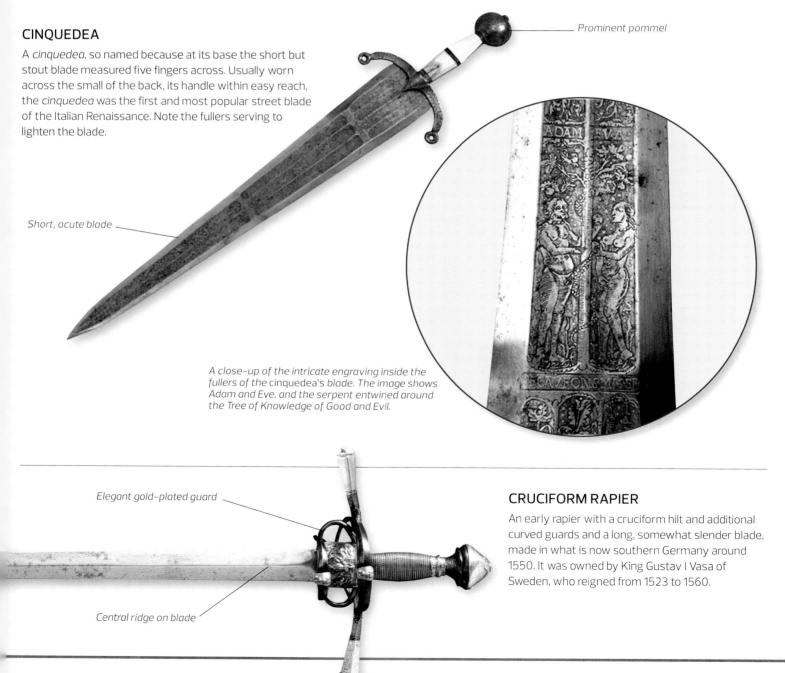

CINQUEDEA

A *cinquedea*, so named because at its base the short but stout blade measured five fingers across. Usually worn across the small of the back, its handle within easy reach, the *cinquedea* was the first and most popular street blade of the Italian Renaissance. Note the fullers serving to lighten the blade.

Prominent pommel

Short, acute blade

A close-up of the intricate engraving inside the fullers of the cinquedea's blade. The image shows Adam and Eve, and the serpent entwined around the Tree of Knowledge of Good and Evil.

Elegant gold-plated guard

CRUCIFORM RAPIER

An early rapier with a cruciform hilt and additional curved guards and a long, somewhat slender blade, made in what is now southern Germany around 1550. It was owned by King Gustav I Vasa of Sweden, who reigned from 1523 to 1560.

Central ridge on blade

The rapier of Gustav I Vasa held properly in the hand. The guard is constructed to protect the entire hand. Note how the index finger is wrapped around the quillon block through the forefinger ring, for secure grip and fine control of the point.

SUMPTUARY LAWS AND CIVILIAN SWORDS

Sumptuary laws—statutes governing civilian dress, often enforcing class distinctions—have always been part of human cultures, but during the Renaissance such laws addressed the novel issue of civilian swords. Ostensibly to prevent young noblemen from bankrupting themselves in search of the most impressive blades and mountings, these laws usually had more to do with keeping the rising merchant class from upstaging the hereditary aristocracy. But they also were intended to discourage street violence. In England under Elizabeth I, statutes forbade the wearing of rapiers with blades longer than "one yard and half a quarter" (about 40 inches) or daggers with blades longer than 12 inches. This was actually a rather strict law, since quite a few rapier blades exceeded the maximum allowed length and had to be "cut down to size."

1550 ÉPÉE

The hilt of a fine civilian sword from about 1550, with a blade by Hernandes Roque of Toledo. Its extremely acute blade would be nearly useless in a heavy battle, but on a street or in a duel, against an unarmored opponent, it would be agile and deadly.

Long crossguard

Narrow thrusting blade

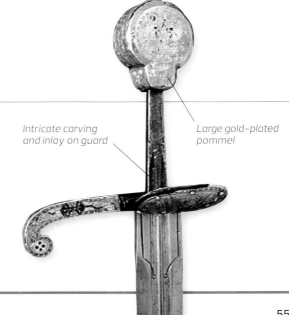

Intricate carving and inlay on guard

Large gold-plated pommel

SINGLE-QUILLON SWORD

A richly decorated but sturdy rapier from the middle of the 16th century, owned by King John III of Sweden. The single quillon, matched with a shell guard to the side, is an uncommon design. Note how the first few inches of the blade are unsharpened, to facilitate wrapping a finger around the quillon for surer control; this stretch of unsharpened blade became known as a ricasso.

The Magnificence of the Renaissance Rapier

The Renaissance rapier is arguably the culmination of the Western sword as both weapon and work of art; these blades are matched in beauty only by the finest Islamic and East Asian swords.

The rapier developed in the 16th century as a civilian sword. Though stout-bladed swords in the style of rapiers became military fixtures, civilian rapiers set the standard for artistry. The word "rapier" probably derives from the Spanish *espada ropera*, or "dress sword," and these weapons became dressy indeed. For the finer examples, blades from Toledo or Solingen, the two legendary blade-forging centers of Europe, would be shipped to artists and master craftsmen

commissioned to fit the blades with intricate and elegant mountings, often in recognizably national and even local styles. The construction of a single sword often involved the handiwork of several craftsmen.

Over the course of the 16th century, the simple cruciform hilt of earlier blades quickly gained complexity and elegance, resulting in the "swept-hilt" style of rapier that became a touchstone in the 16th century. Intricate guards, often with rings and arms that extended forward from the quillons, were matched with a remarkable range of decorated pommels and ornamental scabbards.

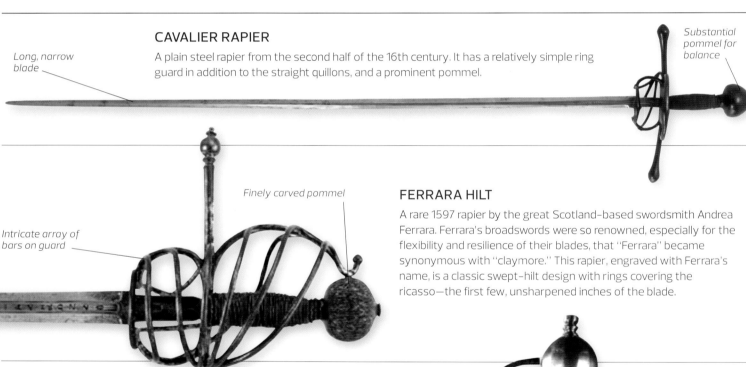

CAVALIER RAPIER

A plain steel rapier from the second half of the 16th century. It has a relatively simple ring guard in addition to the straight quillons, and a prominent pommel.

Long, narrow blade

Substantial pommel for balance

Finely carved pommel

Intricate array of bars on guard

FERRARA HILT

A rare 1597 rapier by the great Scotland-based swordsmith Andrea Ferrara. Ferrara's broadswords were so renowned, especially for the flexibility and resilience of their blades, that "Ferrara" became synonymous with "claymore." This rapier, engraved with Ferrara's name, is a classic swept-hilt design with rings covering the ricasso—the first few, unsharpened inches of the blade.

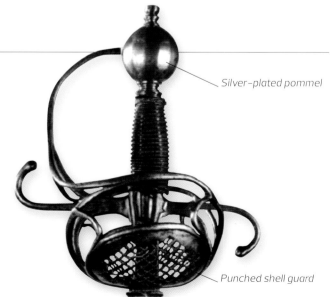

Silver-plated pommel

PICCININO HILT

An elegant hilt by the great Italian swordsmith Antonio Piccinino, from the early 17th century. It displays a graceful sense of balance, between both the punched shell guards and the large pommel and between the two quillons, with their refined curves.

Punched shell guard

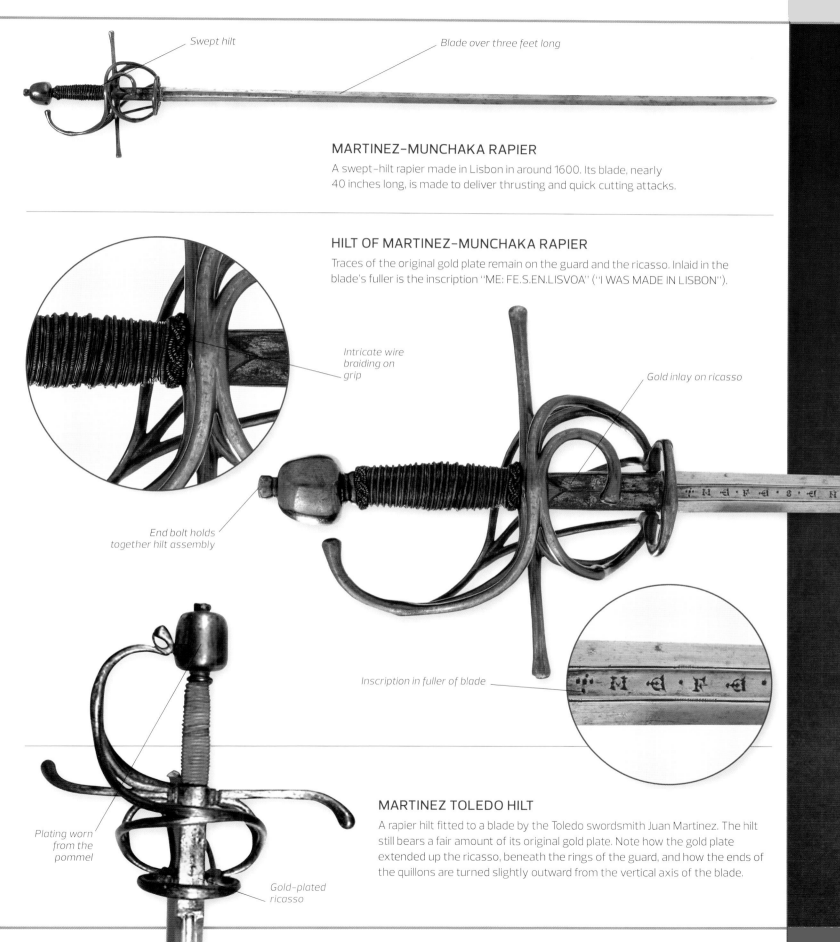

MARTINEZ–MUNCHAKA RAPIER

A swept-hilt rapier made in Lisbon in around 1600. Its blade, nearly
40 inches long, is made to deliver thrusting and quick cutting attacks.

Swept hilt

Blade over three feet long

HILT OF MARTINEZ–MUNCHAKA RAPIER

Traces of the original gold plate remain on the guard and the ricasso. Inlaid in the
blade's fuller is the inscription "ME: FE.S.EN.LISVOA" ("I WAS MADE IN LISBON").

*Intricate wire
braiding on
grip*

Gold inlay on ricasso

*End bolt holds
together hilt assembly*

Inscription in fuller of blade

MARTINEZ TOLEDO HILT

A rapier hilt fitted to a blade by the Toledo swordsmith Juan Martinez. The hilt
still bears a fair amount of its original gold plate. Note how the gold plate
extended up the ricasso, beneath the rings of the guard, and how the ends of
the quillons are turned slightly outward from the vertical axis of the blade.

*Plating worn
from the
pommel*

*Gold-plated
ricasso*

The Rapier and the Art of Fencing

Though fencing had surely existed as a form of training since the advent of the sword, with the popularization of rapiers as civilian swords the sport took on a different cast. Schools of fencing developed around the rapier, each establishing its own recognizable style. The Italians took pride of place throughout the 16th century, and nearly every court in Europe retained an Italian fencing master. In 1567, however, Charles IX of France established the *Académie d'Armes* in Paris; in the following century, the French style of fencing would come to dominate Europe.

Until about the middle of the 17th century, the rapier was seldom used alone. Rather, it was paired with a dagger or short sword, or a small shield called a buckler. Countless noblemen, and others as well, learned the technique of fighting with rapier and dagger. Daggers designed to serve as parrying weapons, often with diamond–shaped blades for strength and stabbing power, developed as complements to the rapier. Known as the *main gauche*, or left hand, because of its supporting role, this type of dagger was often elegantly made and even richly decorated itself.

TOLEDO RAPIER

A relatively restrained 17th–century rapier from Toledo. The straight, cruciform quillons, elegantly functional rings, and long, elegant blade capture the essence of the rapier. The long quillons are a characteristically Spanish touch.

Finely turned grip

Forward ring guard

Acute stabbing point

OFFICER'S RAPIER

An officer's rapier from about 1620, with punched, silver–plated "clamshell" guards at acute angles to the grip, and an openwork pear–shaped pommel. The blade is from Solingen. The wire-wrapped grip was common among Renaissance rapiers.

Punched "clam shell" guard

Openwork pommel

SINGLE–SHELL HILT

An austerely refined German rapier from about 1640, with a slender, four–foot blade and shallow cup guard. Made entirely of steel with no extraneous decoration, this sword is nonetheless as beautiful as it is effective.

Single round shell guard

Button–shaped pommel and quillon ends

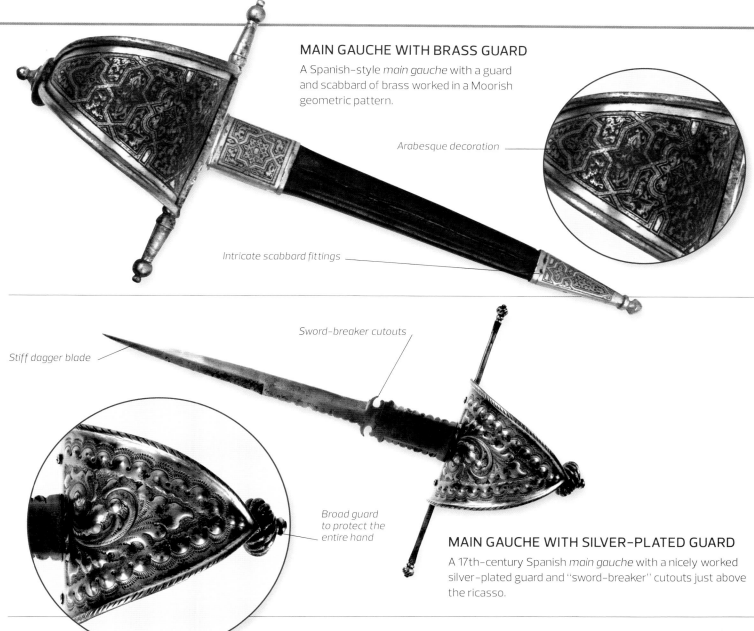

MAIN GAUCHE WITH BRASS GUARD

A Spanish-style *main gauche* with a guard and scabbard of brass worked in a Moorish geometric pattern.

Arabesque decoration

Intricate scabbard fittings

Sword-breaker cutouts

Stiff dagger blade

Broad guard to protect the entire hand

MAIN GAUCHE WITH SILVER-PLATED GUARD

A 17th-century Spanish *main gauche* with a nicely worked silver-plated guard and "sword-breaker" cutouts just above the ricasso.

CALLOT ETCHING

A 1617 etching by Jacques Callot of a duel with rapiers. Here, the rapier serves its primary function: a thrusting attack that runs through the opponent's torso. Note the guard of the sword striking the fatal blow.

THE BLADES OF TOLEDO AND SOLINGEN

Throughout the history of the sword, certain swordmaking centers acquired reputations for excellence. Some became legendary. The most renowned of all European sword sources were Toledo in Spain and Solingen in Germany. Famed for its blades since Roman times, Toledo steel was exceptionally hard and held a keen edge. The fame of Toledo steel extended so far that Toledo blades found their way into the hands of Japanese samurai, who doubtless found a certain caché in Western weapons. Solingen, however, was the most productive source of fine Renaissance blades. Its stature also extended back into antiquity, and even today it remains the center of German knifemaking.

The Triumph of Ornament

As the Renaissance progressed, rapiers became increasingly ornate, and many took the form of presentation swords, meant as badges of honor and status and not as weapons. More practical blades also gained decorative sophistication. Elite swordsmiths and cutlers (who fitted blades with hilts) became celebrities of a sort. Even famed artists, such as Albrecht Dürer, Parmigianino, and Hans Holbein were commissioned to design swords for their patrons. A sword's shell guards and pommel, which were highly visible when the blade was sheathed at the waist, usually received the most artistic attention.

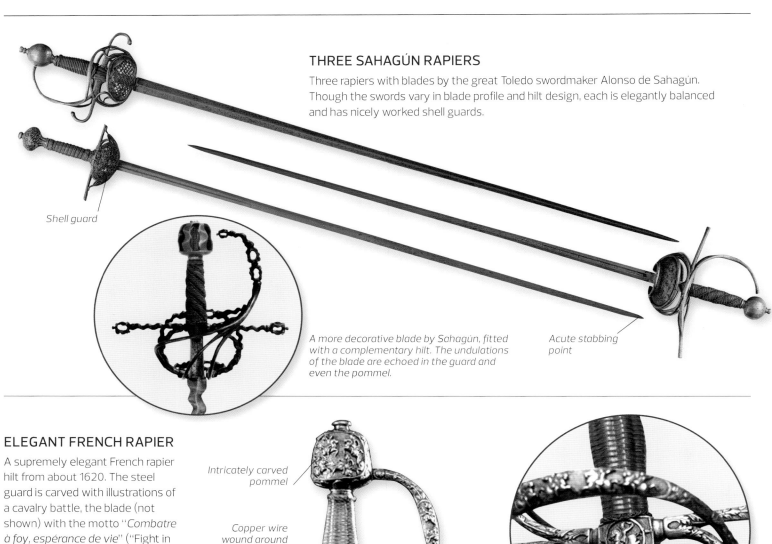

THREE SAHAGÚN RAPIERS

Three rapiers with blades by the great Toledo swordmaker Alonso de Sahagún. Though the swords vary in blade profile and hilt design, each is elegantly balanced and has nicely worked shell guards.

Shell guard

A more decorative blade by Sahagún, fitted with a complementary hilt. The undulations of the blade are echoed in the guard and even the pommel.

Acute stabbing point

ELEGANT FRENCH RAPIER

A supremely elegant French rapier hilt from about 1620. The steel guard is carved with illustrations of a cavalry battle, the blade (not shown) with the motto "Combatre à foy, espérance de vie" ("Fight in faith, hope for life"). Note the large "arms of the hilt"—the guards looping from the quillons to the forward ring guard.

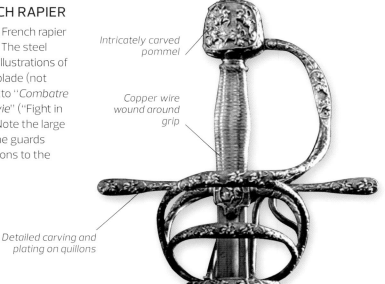

Intricately carved pommel

Copper wire wound around grip

Detailed carving and plating on quillons

A close-up of the guard of the French rapier, showing the sweeping curves of the guard and how finely it depicts a cavalry battle. The quillon block at the base of the blade has a remarkably detailed image of a charging cavalryman.

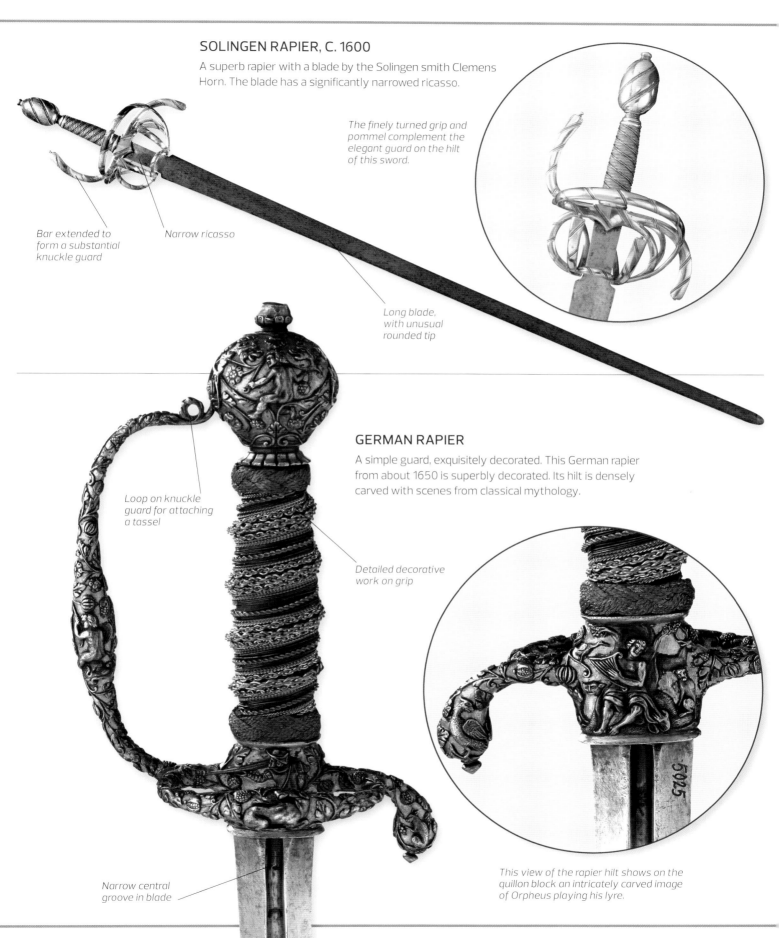

SOLINGEN RAPIER, C. 1600

A superb rapier with a blade by the Solingen smith Clemens Horn. The blade has a significantly narrowed ricasso.

The finely turned grip and pommel complement the elegant guard on the hilt of this sword.

Bar extended to form a substantial knuckle guard

Narrow ricasso

Long blade, with unusual rounded tip

GERMAN RAPIER

A simple guard, exquisitely decorated. This German rapier from about 1650 is superbly decorated. Its hilt is densely carved with scenes from classical mythology.

Loop on knuckle guard for attaching a tassel

Detailed decorative work on grip

Narrow central groove in blade

This view of the rapier hilt shows on the quillon block an intricately carved image of Orpheus playing his lyre.

The Rapiers of Gustavus Adolphus

King Gustav II Adolf, known to history as Gustavus Adolphus, ruled Sweden from 1611 until his death in battle in 1632. He was one of the greatest military minds the world has seen, regarded by many as having invented modern warfare. His aggressive tactics during the Thirty Years' War, based on rapid movement, mobile artillery, and well-integrated and systematically equipped infantry and cavalry, made Sweden a dominant power in Europe. He is the only Swedish ruler allowed the epithet "the Great."

Gustavus Adolphus was not only a great general, he was also a connoisseur of weapons who collected an astonishing array of magnificent swords. The selections presented here form only a small part of his personal collection, which was among the finest in 17th-century Europe. Here are some of the most extraordinary blades ever made.

EQUESTRIAN PORTRAIT OF GUSTAVUS ADOLPHUS

A 17th-century equestrian portrait of Gustavus Adolphus, commemorating his famous victory at the Battle of Breitenfeld in 1631. Gustavus's daring and forward-thinking tactics in that battle led to an overwhelming victory for Protestant forces in the Thirty Years' War. In the portrait, Gustavus holds a rapier with a relatively short but still acute blade.

SHELL GUARD

The shell guard of a magnificent sword originally owned by Gotthard Kettler, the last Master of the Livonian Order of Teutonic Knights. The vermeil decoration shows a finely engraved depiction of an archer on a rearing horse.

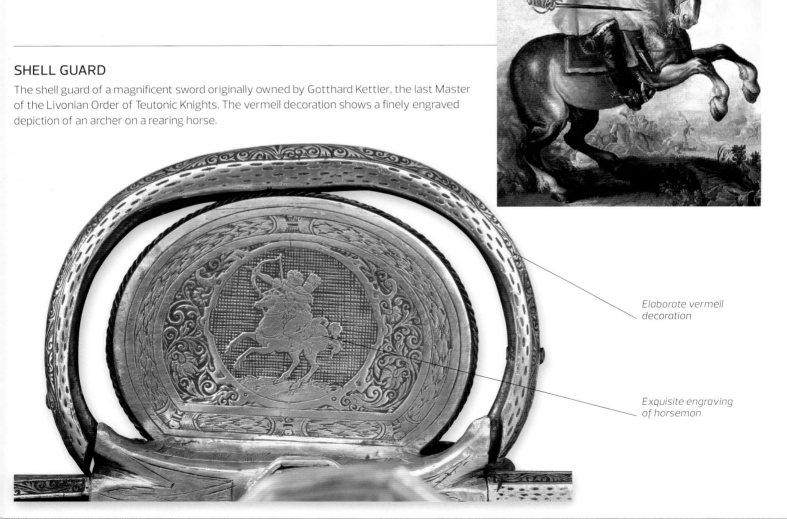

Elaborate vermeil decoration

Exquisite engraving of horseman

The hilt of the Kurland rapier, showing the delicate engraving of birds, flowers, and vines on the guard and the ricasso as well as its faceted pommel. The work is of remarkable quality.

KURLAND RAPIER HILT

The hilt of a magnificent Kurland rapier, made around 1580 and originally owned by Gotthard Kettler. It came into the possession of Gustavus in 1621 during a war with Poland. Its hilt is of steel, covered with gold vermeil engraved with intricate designs.

Faceted pommel

Side ring protecting the ricasso

The shell guard of the Kurland rapier is exquisitely engraved with flowers, scrollwork, and the coat of arms of the Duchy of Kurland, a region of Latvia where Gotthard Kettler was duke.

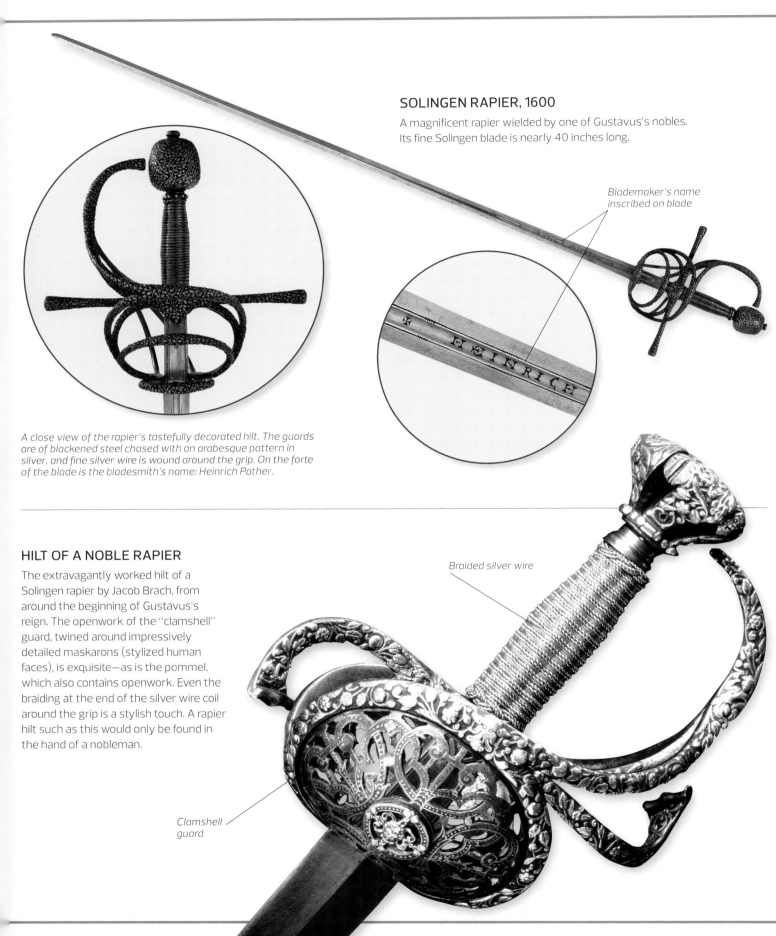

SOLINGEN RAPIER, 1600

A magnificent rapier wielded by one of Gustavus's nobles. Its fine Solingen blade is nearly 40 inches long.

Blademaker's name inscribed on blade

A close view of the rapier's tastefully decorated hilt. The guards are of blackened steel chased with an arabesque pattern in silver, and fine silver wire is wound around the grip. On the forte of the blade is the bladesmith's name: Heinrich Pather.

HILT OF A NOBLE RAPIER

The extravagantly worked hilt of a Solingen rapier by Jacob Brach, from around the beginning of Gustavus's reign. The openwork of the "clamshell" guard, twined around impressively detailed maskarons (stylized human faces), is exquisite—as is the pommel, which also contains openwork. Even the braiding at the end of the silver wire coil around the grip is a stylish touch. A rapier hilt such as this would only be found in the hand of a nobleman.

Braided silver wire

Clamshell guard

LÜTZEN RAPIER

The Solingen-made rapier, signed "Marson," that Gustavus wielded in the 1632 Battle of Lützen, where he met his death. Its acute but sturdy blade was suited for combat.

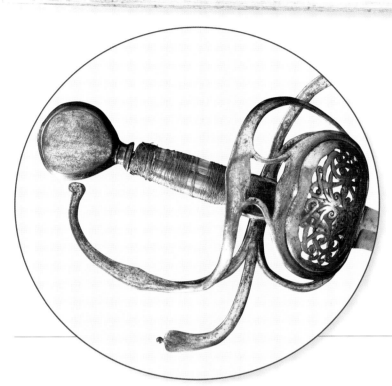

A close image of the elegant but redoubtable hilt of the Lützen rapier. The intricate openwork of the shell guard contrasts with the relatively austere pommel, which is actually flat rather than spherical.

DEATH OF A SOLDIER-KING

Gustavus Adolphus was a brave fighter as well as a gifted general. He was lionized not only for his victories, but also for his tendency to lead cavalry charges at key moments in battles. This was particularly hazardous for Gustavus given that, because of a war wound, he could not wear a steel breastplate, instead using a boiled leather cuirass. In 1632, while leading a charge at the Battle of Lützen in Saxony, Gustavus was isolated in the smoke and confusion of combat, and felled by gunshots. Only when his riderless horse was spotted between the two opposing armies did the truth begin to reveal itself. Though Protestant troops went on to win the battle, the

loss of Gustavus was a major blow to the Protestant cause in the Thirty Years' War. The 1855 painting *The Death of Gustavus Adolphus at the Battle of Lützen* by the Swedish artist Carl Wahlbom shows Gustavus falling from his rearing horse. Though romanticized, the image reveals how the death of Gustavus remained a captivating episode in Swedish and European memory.

A Magnificent Set of Weapons

Gustavus Adolphus owned a remarkable array of rapiers, but none of his weapons were as spectacular as the set he acquired from Bethlen Gábor, also known as Gabriel Bethlen, prince of Transylvania from 1613 until his death in 1629, and briefly (1620–1621) king of Hungary. Like Gustavus, Gábor was a Protestant, and the gift was likely a gesture of solidarity during a time of religious wars in Europe. This matching set of sabre, mace, and dagger was among the most prized possessions in Gustavus's treasury. Richly worked with gold and inlaid with precious stones, these arms are dazzling to behold. But they are not merely ceremonial: both the sabre and the dagger have superb blades made of Damascus steel, the most sought–after blade material in history.

THE GÁBOR DAGGER
With a classic Islamic hilt and a straight Damascus blade, the Gabor Dagger is every bit aas ornate in its mountings as the exquisite sabre.

THE GÁBOR MACE
The Gábor mace is clearly intended to be purely symbolic. While the blades of the other two artifacts are superbly made and theoretically fit for use in battle, the mace is completely plated in gold and encrusted with more than 250 jewels.

DAMASCUS STEEL

One of the great mysteries of swordmaking involves Damascus steel, the extraordinary steel used for centuries to forge blades in India and especially the Middle East. Damascus steel was made from ingots of wootz steel, an alloy apparently first developed in Sri Lanka before being disseminated by trade through India, Persia, and the Middle East. Wootz steel, forged in the style that produced Damascus blades, left mottled patterns in the metal somewhat similar to those of the pattern–welded blades of Europe—but the Damascus blades far excelled those created through ordinary pattern-welding. They held a remarkably hard and sharp cutting edge while retaining a resiliency that made them nearly unbreakable. The precise technique for producing Damascus steel was lost by the 18th century; perhaps because of disruptions in trade cut off the supply of wootz steel to the Middle East. Modern researchers have found evidence that a very specific mix of impurities in the steel contributed to its excellence, but the actual "recipe" is gone.

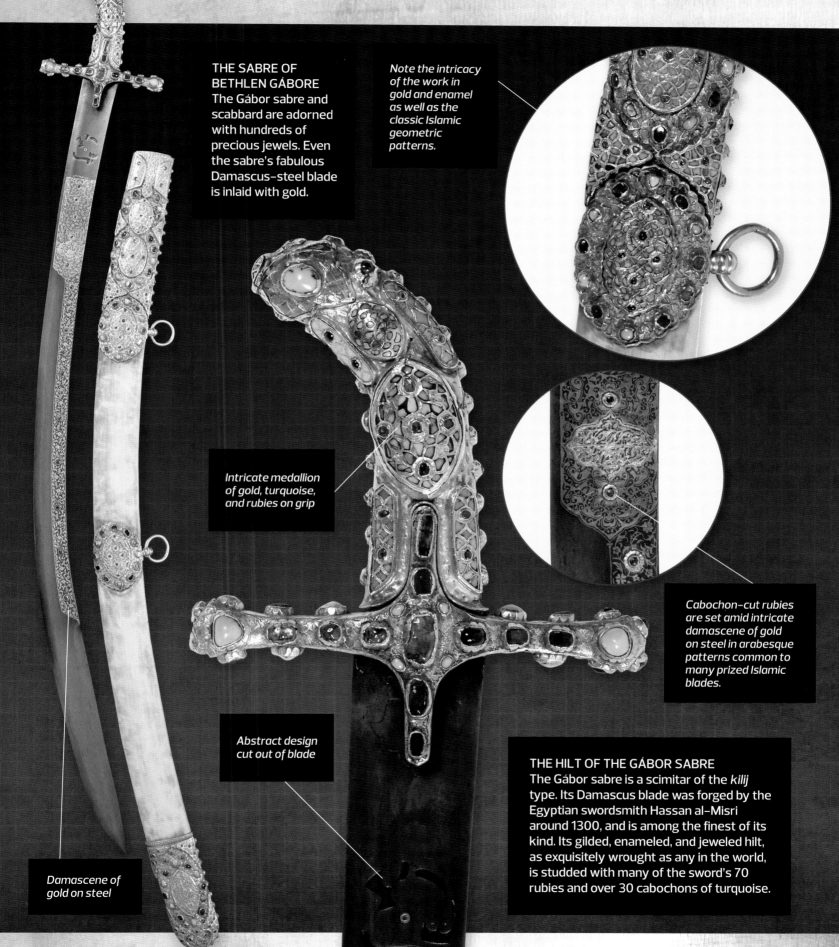

THE SABRE OF BETHLEN GÁBORE
The Gábor sabre and scabbard are adorned with hundreds of precious jewels. Even the sabre's fabulous Damascus–steel blade is inlaid with gold.

Note the intricacy of the work in gold and enamel as well as the classic Islamic geometric patterns.

Intricate medallion of gold, turquoise, and rubies on grip

Cabochon–cut rubies are set amid intricate damascene of gold on steel in arabesque patterns common to many prized Islamic blades.

Abstract design cut out of blade

Damascene of gold on steel

THE HILT OF THE GÁBOR SABRE
The Gábor sabre is a scimitar of the *kilij* type. Its Damascus blade was forged by the Egyptian swordsmith Hassan al–Misri around 1300, and is among the finest of its kind. Its gilded, enameled, and jeweled hilt, as exquisitely wrought as any in the world, is studded with many of the sword's 70 rubies and over 30 cabochons of turquoise.

The Elegance and Ornament of the Dress Rapier

As the 17th century unfolded, rapiers continued to evolve as both weapons and aesthetic objects. War swords and civilian swords continued to diverge in form and style, with single-edged cavalry swords becoming increasingly prominent on the battlefield and narrower, more refined blades predominating elsewhere. The mountings of civilian and especially ceremonial swords became more and more ornate. Civilian swords displayed narrower blades and an increasing use of gadgetry, including hilts fitted with small pistols.

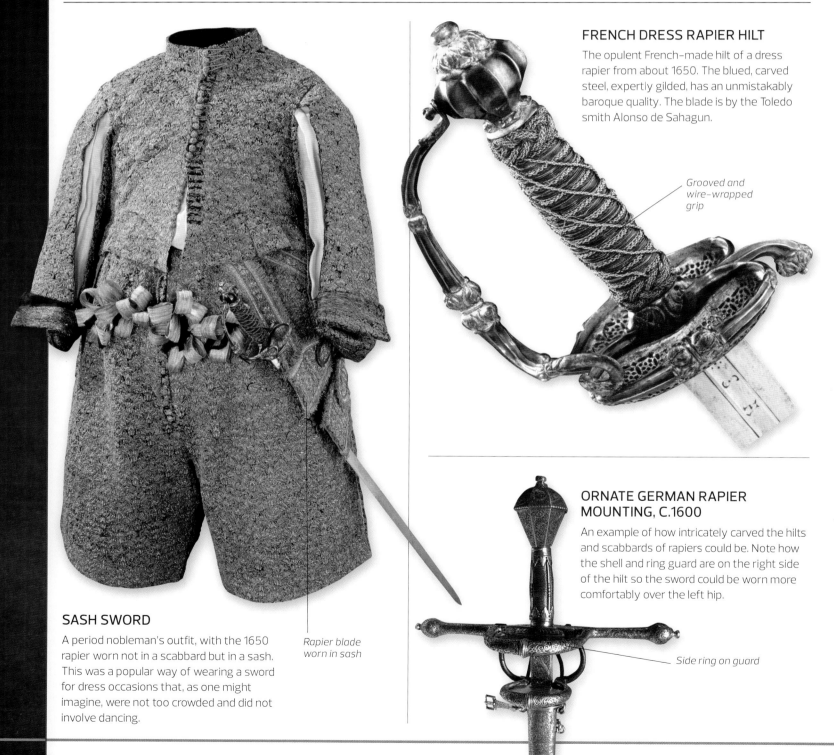

FRENCH DRESS RAPIER HILT

The opulent French-made hilt of a dress rapier from about 1650. The blued, carved steel, expertly gilded, has an unmistakably baroque quality. The blade is by the Toledo smith Alonso de Sahagun.

Grooved and wire-wrapped grip

SASH SWORD

A period nobleman's outfit, with the 1650 rapier worn not in a scabbard but in a sash. This was a popular way of wearing a sword for dress occasions that, as one might imagine, were not too crowded and did not involve dancing.

Rapier blade worn in sash

ORNATE GERMAN RAPIER MOUNTING, C.1600

An example of how intricately carved the hilts and scabbards of rapiers could be. Note how the shell and ring guard are on the right side of the hilt so the sword could be worn more comfortably over the left hip.

Side ring on guard

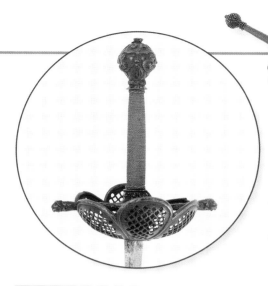

A view of the stylish cruciform hilt, with figured quillon caps and pommel and a guard consisting of six punched shells arranged like the petals of a flower.

COMPOSITE RAPIER

An aristocratic-looking rapier that combines an early 1600s blade by the Solingen smith Johannes Meigen with a later style of hilt. The blade is over 42 inches long, offering formidable reach for its wielder.

Long, refined blade

SPANISH CUP-HILT RAPIER

A classic Spanish cup-hilt rapier of the late 17th century. Note the intricacy of the damascene work on the cup and the extreme delicacy of the knuckle guard.

Intricate damascene work on cup

SOLINGEN CIVILIAN RAPIER

A civilian sword from about 1650 with a Solingen blade. The finials (ends) of the quillons are African heads, and the pommel carved as a lion. The inscription on the blade indicates its origin.

Inscribed "Solingen made me" in Latin

ME FECIT SOLINGEN

Wheel-lock pistol

PISTOL RAPIER

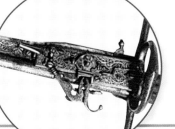

An ornate combination rapier and wheel-lock pistol made around 1580. In addition to the ingenious design, the elaborately engraved pistol barrel and blade mark this as an aristocratic weapon. European noblemen of the period coveted such exotic combination weapons.

Renaissance Pole Arms

In the late medieval period, pole arms—long-shafted weapons with bladed or pointed ends—took on a more vital role in warfare. Armored cavalry had become the scourge of the battlefield, and foot soldiers needed extraordinary protection against the vastly superior speed, height, and mobility of mounted opponents. Eventually, the practice of using pike formations, in which closely-ranked infantry blocks would bristle with pikes up to twenty or more feet long, would become a common countermeasure. This method of using tight formations to repulse cavalry charges would persist, in various forms, through the Napoleonic era.

The most famous pole arms were the halberd and the glaive. Both had multipurpose blades, which often included hooks to pull riders from horses and spikes or axe-blades to penetrate armor. As firearms gained prominence and ease of use in the Renaissance, however, pole arms were largely relegated to ceremonial use, as symbols of power and authority, and became increasingly stylized and ornate.

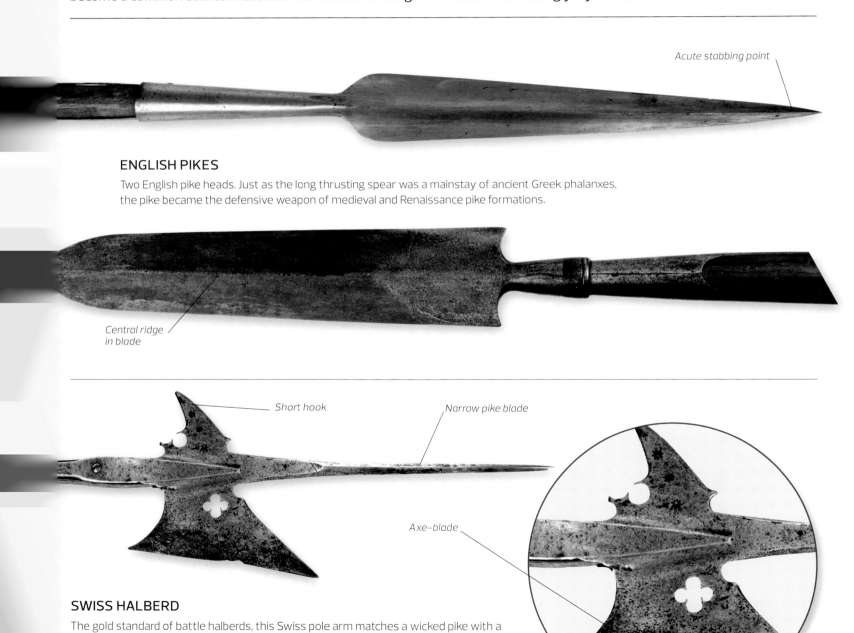

Acute stabbing point

ENGLISH PIKES

Two English pike heads. Just as the long thrusting spear was a mainstay of ancient Greek phalanxes, the pike became the defensive weapon of medieval and Renaissance pike formations.

Central ridge in blade

Short hook

Narrow pike blade

Axe-blade

SWISS HALBERD

The gold standard of battle halberds, this Swiss pole arm matches a wicked pike with a keen axe-blade and short but effective hook. The steel reinforcements along the shaft are there to prevent breakage.

SWISS GUARDS

"Where are my Switzers?" demands the villainous King Claudius in Shakespeare's *Hamlet*, when the vengeful Laertes forces his way into the castle at the head of an angry mob. For centuries, Swiss soldiers were considered the finest mercenaries in Europe, and were used as bodyguards by countless rulers. Often referred to as Swiss Guards, they were typically armed with swords and halberds. The halberds were doubly intimidating, not only because of their symbolic power, but also because the Swiss were the acknowledged masters of the pole arm, and used such weapons with devastating skill. The Swiss reputation for producing world-class mercenaries would continue unabated for centuries; Hessian mercenaries even played a role in the American War of Independence. To this day, the personal guard of the pope is known as the Pontifical Swiss Guard, and consists of exclusively Swiss Catholic recruits. Their motto is *acriter et fideliter*, or "fiercely and faithfully." Privates in the Pontifical Swiss Guard are still called "halberdiers," and pole arms still feature prominently in Vatican pageantry.

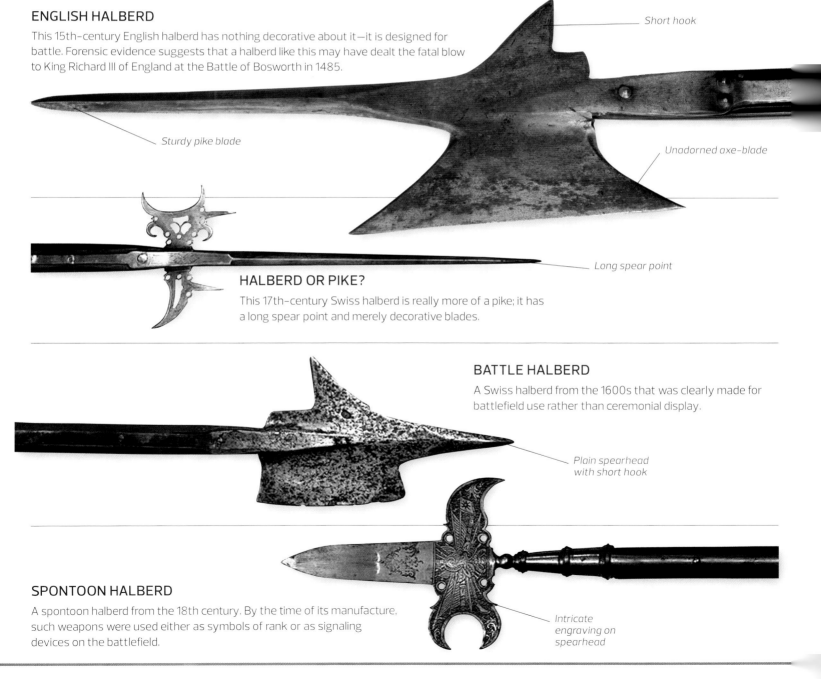

ENGLISH HALBERD

This 15th-century English halberd has nothing decorative about it—it is designed for battle. Forensic evidence suggests that a halberd like this may have dealt the fatal blow to King Richard III of England at the Battle of Bosworth in 1485.

Short hook

Sturdy pike blade

Unadorned axe-blade

Long spear point

HALBERD OR PIKE?

This 17th-century Swiss halberd is really more of a pike; it has a long spear point and merely decorative blades.

BATTLE HALBERD

A Swiss halberd from the 1600s that was clearly made for battlefield use rather than ceremonial display.

Plain spearhead with short hook

SPONTOON HALBERD

A spontoon halberd from the 18th century. By the time of its manufacture, such weapons were used either as symbols of rank or as signaling devices on the battlefield.

Intricate engraving on spearhead

FRENCH POLE ARM

An 18th-century pole arm, symbolic not only in its obviously limited usefulness on the battlefield, but also in its resemblance to the fleur-de-lis, traditional heraldic symbol of the French monarchy.

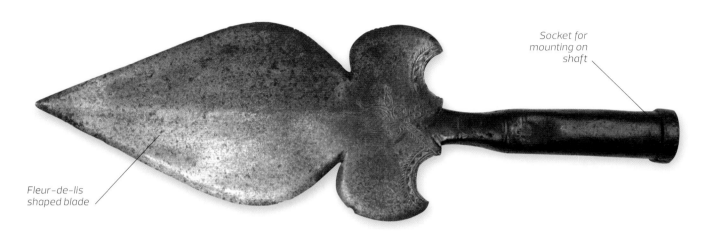

Socket for mounting on shaft

Fleur-de-lis shaped blade

SWISS POLE ARM

The finely incised head of a Swiss pole arm, most likely used as a symbol of rank on the battlefield. Of all the soldiers in Europe, the Swiss were most feared for their skill with pole arms.

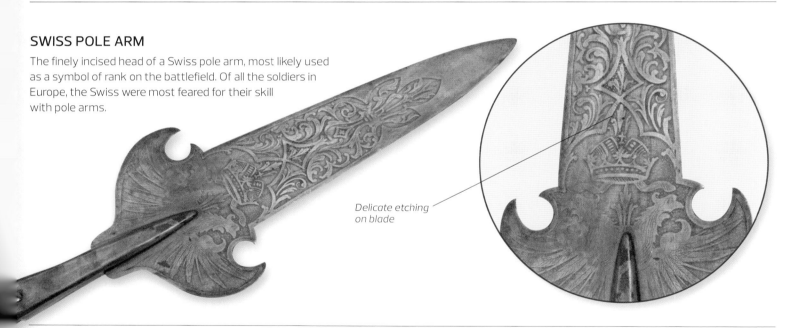

Delicate etching on blade

CEREMONIAL POLE ARM

A richly decorated halberd for the honor guard of Holy Roman Emperor Maximilian II. Made in 1571 by Hans Stromai of Augsburg, it depicts, among other motifs, the double-headed eagle of the Holy Roman Empire.

Axe-head inscribed with double-headed eagle

ITALIAN POLE ARM

An ornately decorated, probably ceremonial Italian glaive, or *fouchard*, in which a long, single-edged blade is supplemented by two hooks used to take down horsemen.

Long, single-edged blade

PARTISAN

The partisan, or *partizan*, was typically a pike with axe-blades fixed below its point. As in this later example, the axe-blades eventually gave way to decorative flourishes, though the pike blade remained.

Decorative "axe-blades"

17TH-CENTURY HALBERD

A halberd from the bodyguard of the prince of Liechtenstein, made in 1632. It is beautifully worked, and its manufacture date is actually engraved in the hook portion of the blade.

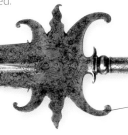

Intricate commemorative engraving on blade

YEOMEN OF THE GUARD

The Yeomen of the Guard are one of the personal bodyguards of the British monarch. The guard was established by Henry Tudor before his defeat of Richard III at the Battle of Bosworth in 1485, after which he became King Henry VII and inaugurated the Tudor dynasty. To this day, the 60 members of the Yeomen of the Guard, drawn from retired British military personnel, wear Tudor uniforms and carry ceremonial pole arms—in this case, glaives, also known as *fouchards*. Interestingly, for centuries, naval personnel were banned from joining the Yeomen of the Guard because they take oaths of loyalty to the Admiralty rather than the Crown, but this rule has since been dropped. The Captain of the Yeomen of the Guard is the traditionally the Deputy Chief Whip of the House of Lords.

Maces and Axes from the Renaissance Onwards

The mace, which had become a prominent battlefield weapon following the advent of plate armor, also became a more symbolic weapon as firearms gradually made armor obsolete. Many examples from the late Renaissance and after are richly decorated, and sometimes oversized, for use as symbols of authority, tradition, and solemnity. Regular battle-axes, as opposed to halberds, became even more scarce, but some interesting examples remain. By the 19th century, any pretense of battlefield use had been dropped.

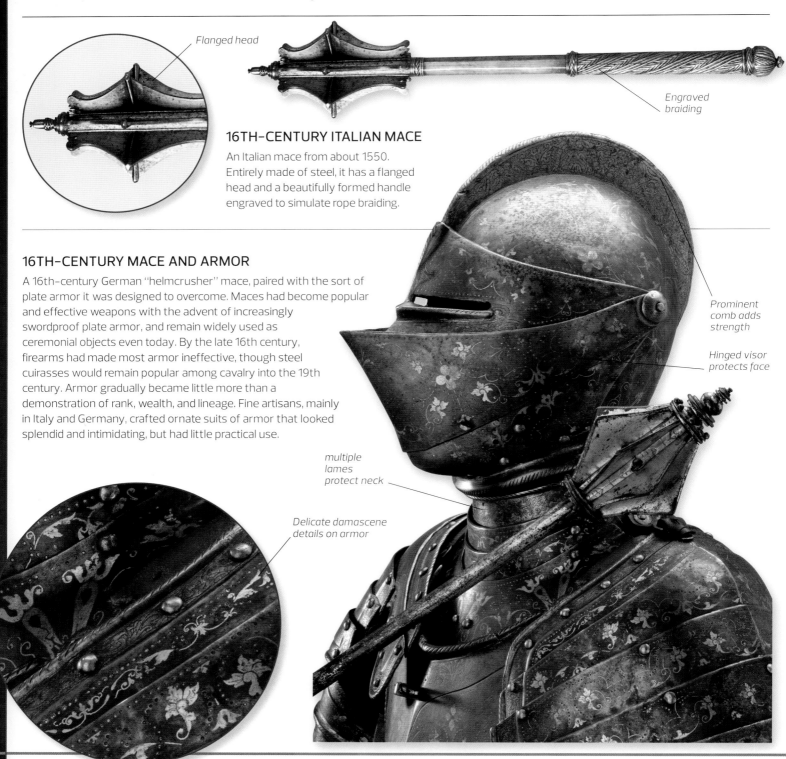

Flanged head

Engraved braiding

16TH-CENTURY ITALIAN MACE

An Italian mace from about 1550. Entirely made of steel, it has a flanged head and a beautifully formed handle engraved to simulate rope braiding.

16TH-CENTURY MACE AND ARMOR

A 16th-century German "helmcrusher" mace, paired with the sort of plate armor it was designed to overcome. Maces had become popular and effective weapons with the advent of increasingly swordproof plate armor, and remain widely used as ceremonial objects even today. By the late 16th century, firearms had made most armor ineffective, though steel cuirasses would remain popular among cavalry into the 19th century. Armor gradually became little more than a demonstration of rank, wealth, and lineage. Fine artisans, mainly in Italy and Germany, crafted ornate suits of armor that looked splendid and intimidating, but had little practical use.

Prominent comb adds strength

Hinged visor protects face

multiple lames protect neck

Delicate damascene details on armor

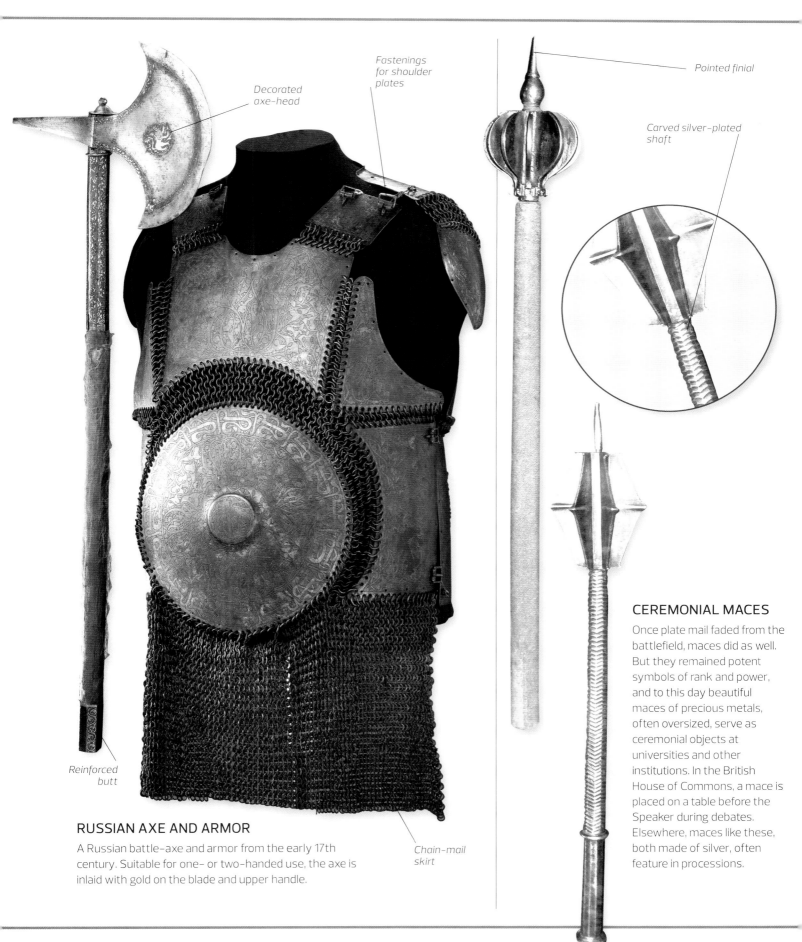

Decorated axe-head

Fastenings for shoulder plates

Pointed finial

Carved silver-plated shaft

Reinforced butt

RUSSIAN AXE AND ARMOR

A Russian battle-axe and armor from the early 17th century. Suitable for one- or two-handed use, the axe is inlaid with gold on the blade and upper handle.

Chain-mail skirt

CEREMONIAL MACES

Once plate mail faded from the battlefield, maces did as well. But they remained potent symbols of rank and power, and to this day beautiful maces of precious metals, often oversized, serve as ceremonial objects at universities and other institutions. In the British House of Commons, a mace is placed on a table before the Speaker during debates. Elsewhere, maces like these, both made of silver, often feature in processions.

The Age of the Sabre

The Twilight of the Western Sword

The story of the Western sword from the 18th century to our own is one of increasing marginalization. As firearms and even more destructive weapons came to dominate not only battlefields but also dueling and sports, the sword became less and less a weapon, and more and more a symbol. Nevertheless, the 18th and 19th centuries saw a last, spectacular flourishing of the sword on the battlefields of Europe and its empires, as well as America: this was the golden age of the sabre. Also, ceremonial swords of all kinds have continued to serve as cultural icons.

AN 1891 PAINTING of a cavalry charge by French hussars at the Battle of Friedland in 1807. The officer in the foreground wields a Turkish-style sabre.

From Rapier to Small Sword

The trend toward civilian use that characterized the late development of the rapier led to increasing refinement—and decreasing blade length. By the middle of the 17th century, aristocratic men of France and the Low Countries had begun carrying a lighter, shorter form of rapier. In Germany especially, swordsmiths began experimenting with different kinds of blades. Some of those blades were broad and strong at the forte (hilt end) for parrying but tapered or even stepped down to an extremely acute point for lethal thrusting and quick cutting attacks.

Another type of blade, which became very popular, was hollow ground, with a triangular cross section, such that it was both light and exceptionally strong. Often, these blades were fitted to hilts with double-shell guards; the blade would pass through an opening at the center of the guard. This is the classic small sword, and it would become the standard gentleman's sword until the end of the 18th century. Its lightness, quick tip, stiff blade, and tremendous penetration made it deadly in the hand of many a duelist from the late 17th century into the 19th.

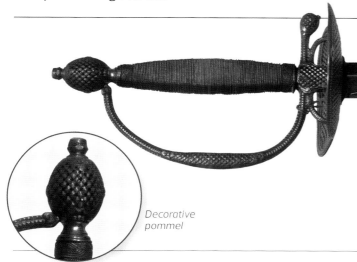

Blade "stepped" down from wide base to narrow thrusting blade

COLICHEMARDE

A transitional form of sword called a *colichemarde*, which may be a French rendering of the title of Johann Phillip, the Count of Konigsmark, a well-known mercenary of the mid-17th century. The blade is broad and stout toward the hilt for parrying but steps down to a much narrower tip for quick, deadly thrusts.

Decorative pommel

Stiff, acute blade with central ridge

1701 RAPIER

A transitional rapier from 1701, with a hollow-ground, slightly shorter than normal blade with a diamond cross section.

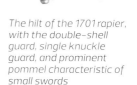

The hilt of the 1701 rapier, with the double-shell guard, single knuckle guard, and prominent pommel characteristic of small swords

Large, ornate crossguard ends

Hollow-ground blade

"PILLOW SWORD"

An ornately hilted "pillow sword," meant for keeping by one's bed for self-defense, from the late 17th century. Note how the hollow-ground blade, with a triangular cross section designed purely for parrying and thrusting, is essentially that of a small sword.

The Emergence of the Western Sabre

The word "sabre" covers a vast range of swords, but has come to be most closely associated with curved, single-edged blades, predominantly those meant for use by cavalry. The word itself probably originated as Turkish and found its way into Western European languages by way of Eastern European use, especially by the Hungarians, Russians, and Poles.

The earliest iconic sabres of Europe were those of the superb Polish cavalry of the 17th and 18th centuries. The classic Polish sabre, which resembled those of the Ottoman Turks, was called a *szabla*. A lighter, shorter version, made for fighting on foot as well as horseback, was called a *karabela*. Both swords typically had a simple cross hilt with angled knuckle guard, a rather short grip, and minimal pommel.

Central fuller to stiffen and lighten blade

Islamic-style crossguard

KARABELA

A classic Polish *karabela* from the mid-18th century, with its cross hilt and gently curved blade, meant mainly for slashing but also suitable for thrusting.

POLISH SABRE WITH KNUCKLE GUARD

The hilt of a classic *szabla* from 1650.
The simple, functional hilt is all business.

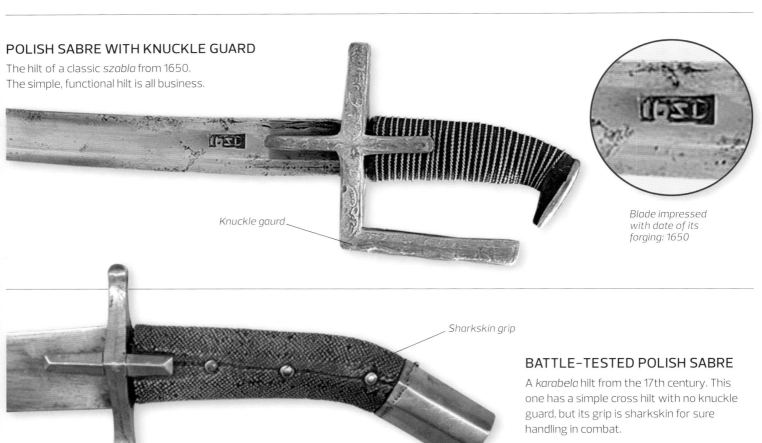

Knuckle gaurd

Blade impressed with date of its forging: 1650

Sharkskin grip

BATTLE-TESTED POLISH SABRE

A *karabela* hilt from the 17th century. This one has a simple cross hilt with no knuckle guard, but its grip is sharkskin for sure handling in combat.

Carved
walnut
grip

Plain steel
cruciform guard

NARVA KARABELA HILT

The elegant hilt of a *karabela* owned by the
Russian general Charles Eugéne de Cröy, captured
by Swedish troops in the Battle of Narva in 1700.

Central fuller
to stiffen and
lighten blade

Islamic-style
crossguard

Slightly rounded
blade point

Horn grip

KARABELA WITH HORN GRIP

A sturdy, all-business Polish *karabela* from the
17th century. As its somewhat rounded tip indicates,
it was made purely for slashing from horseback.

THE BATTLE OF NARVA

In 1700, young King Charles XII of Sweden found himself
tested by a triple alliance of Peter the Great of Russia,
Augustus the Strong of Saxony-Poland-Lithuania, and

Frederick IV of Denmark-Norway. Peter the Great would,
in the coming years, modernize the Russian military
considerably, but in 1700 it was still far less well drilled and
battle-ready than the Swedish army. And the young Swedish
king was a modern strategic thinker himself. Despite his
youth, Charles proved an able tactician, and won decisive
victories early on in what became the Great Northern War. At
Narva, on the border of Estonia and Russia, Charles defeated
a Russian army three to four times larger than his own. As the
armies faced each other in a blinding snowstorm, Charles
waited for the wind to shift so that the snow blew in the eyes
of Russian troops, and then attacked, his forces in two
columns. The Russian lines broke, and in their retreat
thousands were killed when a bridge collapsed. The Russian
general, Charles Eugéne de Cröy, was captured. Though King
Charles of Sweden would eventually make the critical mistake
of invading Russia and losing the war, the Battle of Narva
remains a storied military victory—as many as 18,000 Russian
soldiers died, and fewer than 1,000 Swedes.

Classic Battle Sabres

In the 18th century, the sabre became the preferred blade for cavalry, whether light or heavy. Even dragoons—horsemen who primarily bore firearms—were equipped with sabres for the melee that often followed gunfire. The glorious cavalry charge, that iconic image of the glory and fury of war, often was a matter of bearing down on enemy ranks with sabres in hand.

By the late 18th century, the debate over the most effective form of sabre had largely come down to a question of blade curvature. A curved blade allowed for slashing strokes to be delivered on the move, without the problem of having to withdraw a thrust before using the sword again to parry or strike. But straight blades, especially two-edged ones, had their advocates as well. In the Napoleonic Wars, the debate would take on moral overtones: French cavalrymen objected to the 1796 pattern British heavy cavalry sword as too brutal a weapon for civilized warfare. Their complaints went unheeded.

1796 PATTERN SWORD

The most brutal of sabres, the 1796 British heavy cavalry sword. A "backsword," with a thick, stiff spine opposite its single edge, this heavy sword fell like an axe—wielding it involved little or no finesse.

Reinforced scabbard for durability in campaigns

Openwork guard

HILT OF 1796 PATTERN OFFICER'S SWORD

The hilt of a 1796 pattern British heavy cavalry officer's sword. While the blade is similar to that of the regular sword, the hilt is much more ornate, with an elaborate openwork bowl guard.

FRENCH SABRE HILT C.1770

A classic Islamic-style French sabre hilt from about 1770. The style of the hilt, which unites Islamic and Western elements, suits the blade, which, as its decoration reveals, is in fact Turkish.

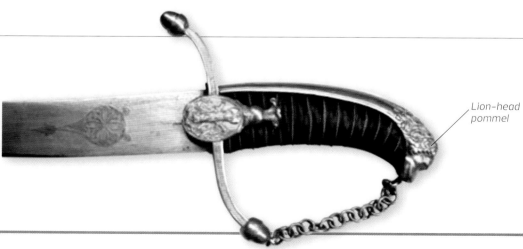

Lion-head pommel

THE HUSSARS

Hussars were the most romanticized cavalry of Europe from the16th through 19th centuries. Originating in Hungary in the early 1500s, they were at first irregular light cavalry, but were soon organized into Ottoman-style units and used to scout, harass enemy troops, and occasionally charge opposing formations. The practice spread to Poland, whose hussars became the gold standard of European cavalry in the 17th and 18th centuries. While a more heavily armored and armed version of the hussars gained glory in Central Europe, the lighter, more dashing style of hussar dominated in Western Europe, and it was these hussars who became the icons of mounted warfare in the Napoleonic era. They were the most highly maneuverable military units, and often undertook the tasks of scouting and harrying enemy forces. As if their splendid uniforms were not enough, it was considered de rigeur for hussars to have stylish mustaches. The hussars' reputation for reckless bravery was such that Napoleon himself remarked that he never expected a hussar to live past the age of thirty.

TWO SABRE HILTS

Two European sabres from the early 19th century. The one above has an unadorned "stirrup" hilt, with a single squared knuckle guard resembling a stirrup. The one below is far more ornate, with a swept three-bar hilt and an Islamic blade of Damascus steel.

Stirrup hilt

Three- bar hilt

FRENCH HUSSAR SENIOR OFFICER SABRE

The elegant sabre of a senior officer of the French hussars (light cavalry) under Napoleon. Note how the curve of the blade allows for both slashing and thrusting attacks.

Richly appointed scabbard

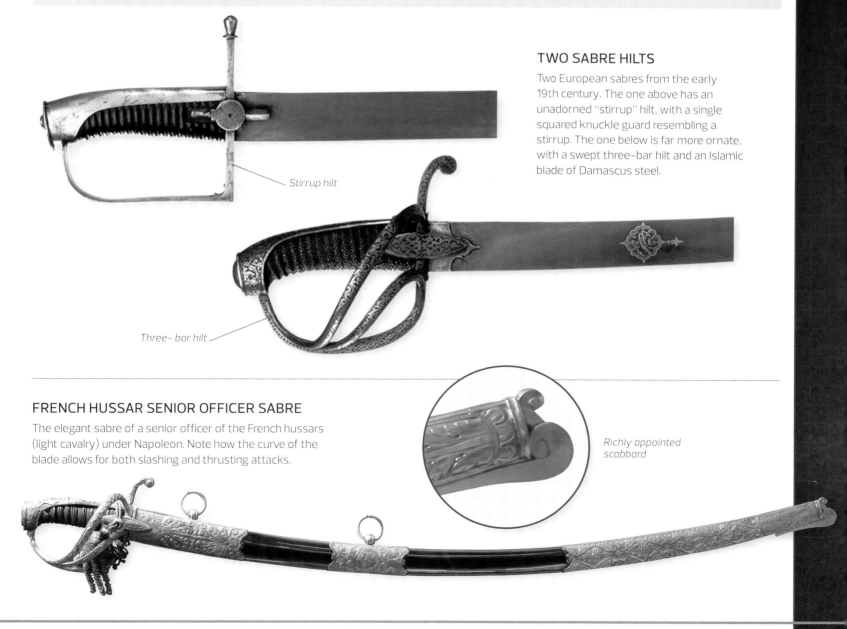

Sabres of Napoleonic Leaders

The Napoleonic Wars, from Napoleon's coup d'état in 1799 through his final defeat at Waterloo in 1815, transformed warfare. Mass conscription led to massive armies, which faced each other with a powerful array of weapons and whose generals had to master new forms of strategy and tactics. For all that, the sword remained a prominent weapon, both in the hands of soldiers—especially cavalry—and adorning the uniforms of generals and other leaders.

Many of Napoleon's generals, including most famous Marshals, used sabres of Islamic origin, some of which were acquired during Napoleon's campaign in Egypt in 1798.

NEY'S SABRE
The sabre of Michel Ney, with its wickedly curved blade, widening noticeably toward the point is characteristic of 14th–16th-century Ottoman and Egyptian swords.

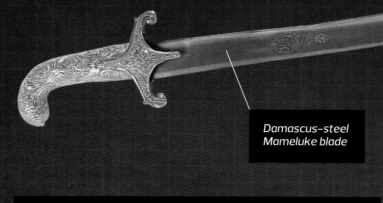

Damascus–steel Mameluke blade

THREE DISTINGUISHED NAPOLEONIC SABRES
On the left, a sabre of Prussian Field Marshal Gebhard von Blücher. In the center, a sabre of Marshal Michel Ney, one of Napoleon's ablest commanders. On the right, a saber of Jean Baptiste Kléber, perhaps Napoleon's most talented lieutenant until his death by an assassin's hand in 1800. The sabres of both Ney and Kléber have Egyptian blades and were doubtless acquired during Napoleon's Egyptian campaign.

MASSENA'S SABRE
An Islamic-bladed sabre of Marshal André Masséna, who served as one of Napoleon's most trusted generals through much of the Napoleonic Wars.

MOREAU'S SABRE
A sabre of Jean Victor Marie Moreau, a French general who assisted Napoleon in his 1799 coup but later turned against him. He eventually died from wounds received while advising forces arrayed against Napoleon in 1813.

NAPOLEON'S SABRE
The hilt of a sabre, dating from about 1800, which belonged to Napoleon himself. In its combination of a simple stirrup hilt and ornate, even imperial decoration, it suits its owner, who was crowned Emperor of France in 1804.

CLOSE-UP OF MOREAU'S SABRE
HILT: The elegant hilt of Moreau's sabre. Though simple in overall form, with one short forward quillon, a single knuckle guard, and a badge at the quillon block, it is very richly carved. The blade is inlaid with the Muslim *Shahada*, or statement of faith ("There is no God but God, and Mohammed is His Prophet"), and the name of the swordsmith: Amal Hadj Songkor.

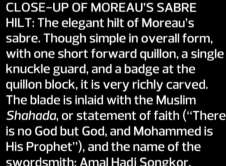

THE DEATH AND LIFE OF MICHEL NEY

In 1815, Marshal Michel Ney, a lieutenant Napoleon had commended as "the bravest of the brave," was shot by a firing squad in Paris as an example to other high-ranking veterans of Napoleon's reign. Or was he? A court martial assembled before had refused to condemn Ney, who was adored by his troops and a hero to many French. Some evidence suggests that, with the aid of French and foreign friends, Ney's execution was faked and he was spirited out of the country to begin a new life in America.

Embellishing the Military Sabre

As the 19th century unfolded, sabres not only served as a means of indicating rank; they also became a way for soldiers to add a bit of dash or personalization to their uniform. While regular troops were mostly limited to modifying the points of their weapons, many officers customized their weapons' fittings.

Most officers owned multiple swords, including at least one for battle and one for ceremonial dress. Ceremonial dress swords were usually richly appointed, with more slender blades and commemorative inscriptions or other, often highly elaborate, embellishments. Generals, of course, had the most impressive swords.

Ornately carved, gold-plated pommel

BEAUHARNAIS SABRE HILT

The regal hilt of a sabre owned by Eugène de Beauharnais, stepson of Napoleon and Viceroy of Italy during his stepfather's reign as Emperor of France. The simple guard's two quillons end in hounds' heads; the head at the end of the rear quillon connects by a gold chain to the mouth of the lion's head pommel. Another lion's head adorns the quillon block.

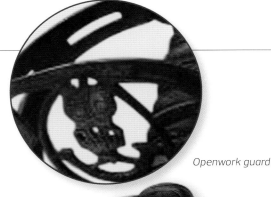

Openwork guard

THREE GOTHIC HILT SABRES

Three British "Gothic" hilt sabres from the middle of the 19th century. Though not considered especially effective combat weapons, they had graceful, visually appealing hilts.

Understated, functional pommel

Stout ricasso for a finger wrapped over the guard

Counterguard to protect the inside of the hand

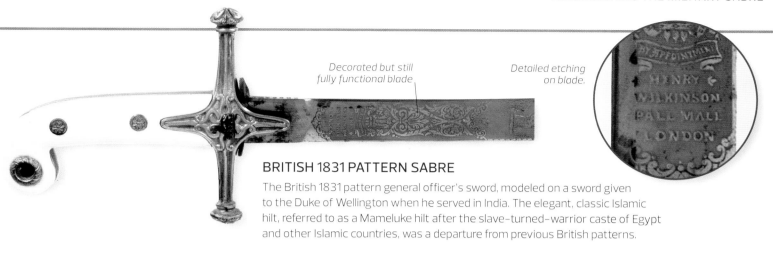

Decorated but still fully functional blade

Detailed etching on blade.

BRITISH 1831 PATTERN SABRE

The British 1831 pattern general officer's sword, modeled on a sword given to the Duke of Wellington when he served in India. The elegant, classic Islamic hilt, referred to as a Mameluke hilt after the slave–turned–warrior caste of Egypt and other Islamic countries, was a departure from previous British patterns.

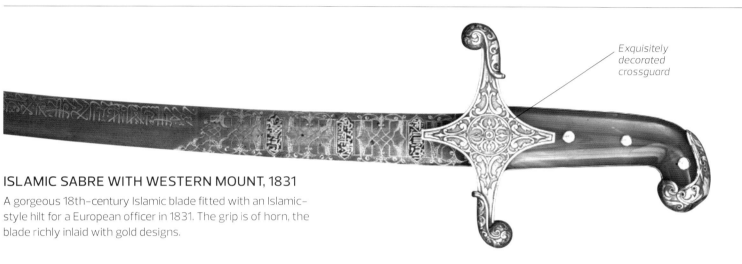

Exquisitely decorated crossguard

ISLAMIC SABRE WITH WESTERN MOUNT, 1831

A gorgeous 18th–century Islamic blade fitted with an Islamic-style hilt for a European officer in 1831. The grip is of horn, the blade richly inlaid with gold designs.

Lion–head pommel

SWEDISH INFANTRY OFFICER'S SWORD

A 1859 Swedish infantry officer's sabre. Its sharkskin grip is enclosed within a beautifully gilded and enameled hilt with the arms of Sweden and Norway. Typically, the guard is asymmetrical, much more narrow on the left side of the grip to facilitate wearing on the right side of the body.

Gold back plate on grip

Sharkskin grip

Plain steel scabbard for battlefield use

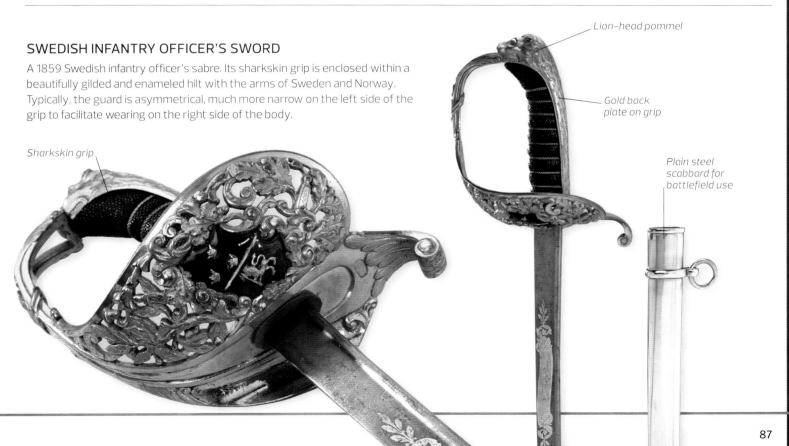

The Late Western Sabre

In the middle to late 19th century and into the early 20th century, sabres became less and less effective on the battlefield, and officers' swords in particular became elaborate indicators of rank and distinction. Though massed cavalry charges figured in both the Crimean War of 1853–1856 and the Franco–Prussian war of 1870–71, such tactics were already becoming a thing of the past.

Nonetheless, the sabre continued to be forged and refined. The British 1908 pattern cavalry sabre is considered by many to be the finest sword for its purpose ever designed, and the "Patton sabre," designed for U.S. cavalry by then–lieutenant George S. Patton in 1913, was very similar. Both swords, however, found little use in the field.

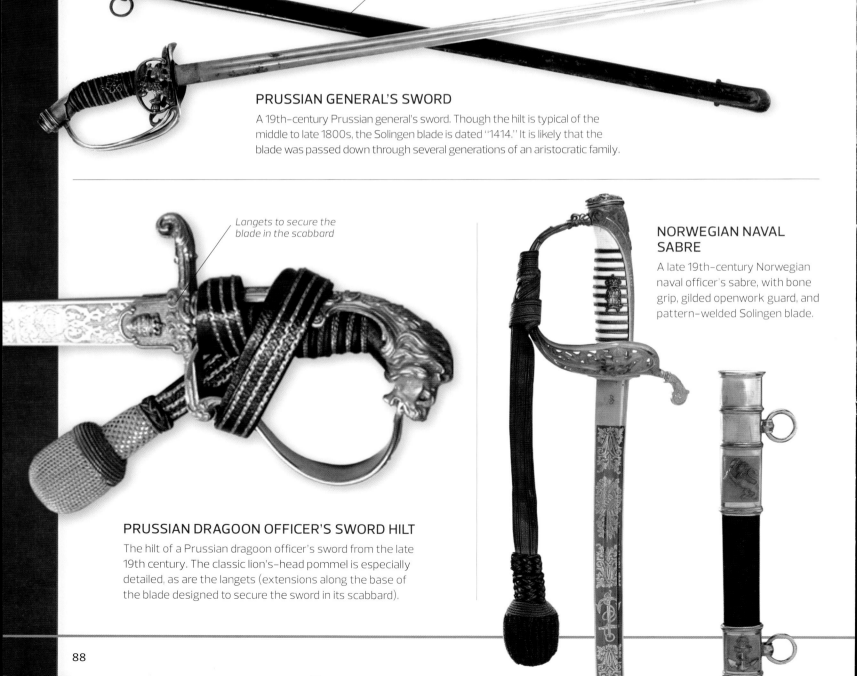

Understated, functional and durable scabbard

PRUSSIAN GENERAL'S SWORD

A 19th-century Prussian general's sword. Though the hilt is typical of the middle to late 1800s, the Solingen blade is dated "1414." It is likely that the blade was passed down through several generations of an aristocratic family.

Langets to secure the blade in the scabbard

NORWEGIAN NAVAL SABRE

A late 19th-century Norwegian naval officer's sabre, with bone grip, gilded openwork guard, and pattern-welded Solingen blade.

PRUSSIAN DRAGOON OFFICER'S SWORD HILT

The hilt of a Prussian dragoon officer's sword from the late 19th century. The classic lion's-head pommel is especially detailed, as are the langets (extensions along the base of the blade designed to secure the sword in its scabbard).

EDWARD VII NAVAL SABRE

A naval officer's sabre owned by Britain's King Edward VII. The splendid hilt, with its lion's-head pommel and carved and gilded brass guard, is typical of much of the 19th century. The blade is slightly curved, and single-edged except for the last nine inches, which are double-edged.

Lion's head pommel

Ornamental tassel for dress occasions

Bowl guard of sheet steel

BRITISH 1908 PATTERN CAVALRY SABRE

The British 1908 pattern cavalry sabre, considered by many experts the best-designed military sword of all time. After much debate, designers settled on a straight, stiff blade meant almost exclusively for thrusting. Behind the substantial bowl guard, the pistol grip is designed to align the sword ergonomically for effective thrusting.

Slender blade with wide fuller

GERMAN IMPERIAL SABRE

A German cavalry sabre from the First World War. It is a functional weapon, with a simple stirrup hilt and slightly curved blade, and it was of little use on the battlefield.

Ornately carved guard

Acute thrusting blade

Eagle-head pommel

19TH-CENTURY FRENCH OFFICER'S SABRE

This regal French officer's sabre is adorned with imperial imagery of a Marine officer's dress uniform.

Dress and Presentation Swords

As the sword's utility on the battlefield began to dwindle, its stature as an item of beauty and prestige increased. Though, after the early years of the 19th century, men very seldom wore swords as part of their ordinary dress, they did take them up for important ceremonial occasions. Dress swords, whether based on small swords, rapiers, or sabres, were often objects of beauty and fascination.

The same has remained true of presentation swords. Swords became ritual objects, bound up with martial traditions and court ceremonies. To this day, swords are often given as civilian awards, the implication often being that the recipient has contributed significantly to sustaining the cultural or economic stature of a nation. Such swords are often made using materials quite unsuitable for the battlefield.

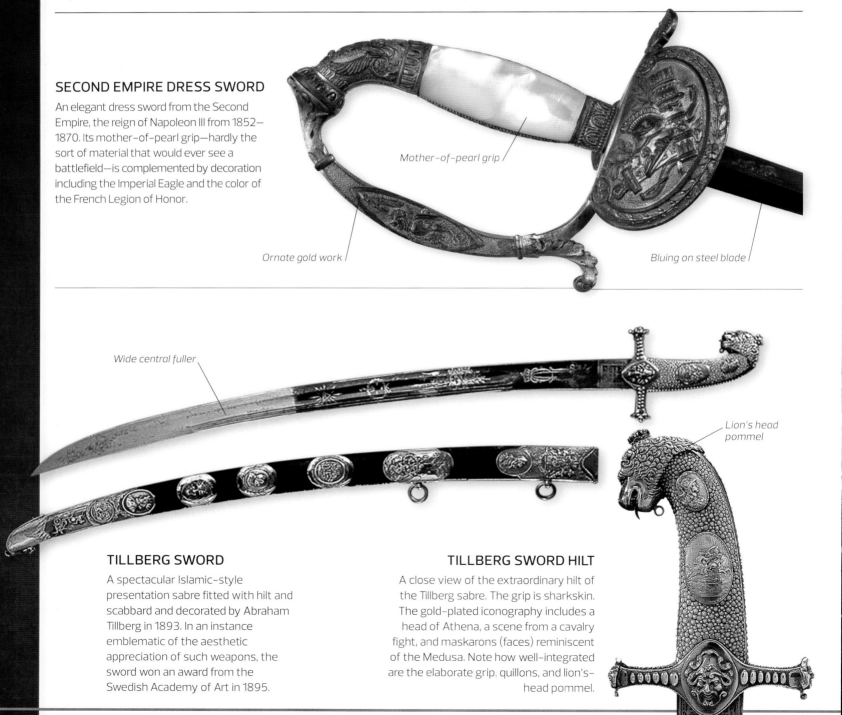

SECOND EMPIRE DRESS SWORD

An elegant dress sword from the Second Empire, the reign of Napoleon III from 1852–1870. Its mother-of-pearl grip—hardly the sort of material that would ever see a battlefield—is complemented by decoration including the Imperial Eagle and the color of the French Legion of Honor.

Mother-of-pearl grip

Ornate gold work

Bluing on steel blade

Wide central fuller

Lion's head pommel

TILLBERG SWORD

A spectacular Islamic-style presentation sabre fitted with hilt and scabbard and decorated by Abraham Tillberg in 1893. In an instance emblematic of the aesthetic appreciation of such weapons, the sword won an award from the Swedish Academy of Art in 1895.

TILLBERG SWORD HILT

A close view of the extraordinary hilt of the Tillberg sabre. The grip is sharkskin. The gold-plated iconography includes a head of Athena, a scene from a cavalry fight, and maskarons (faces) reminiscent of the Medusa. Note how well-integrated are the elaborate grip, quillons, and lion's-head pommel.

Grip engraved with the owner's Masonic rank of thirty-third level

Blade etched with its owner's name and Masonic symbols

MASON'S DRESS SWORD

An ornate dress sword worn by Charles Comstock, an American Freemason who had attained the 33rd degree, the highest in the Order. The sword was custom manufactured by a firm in Cincinnati.

Ornate scabbard decoration

KING OF SIAM'S SABRE

A fine presentation sabre made by the Wilkinson Sword Company for presentation to King Chulalongkorn (1853–1910) of Siam. The hilt is silver, with an ivory grip and an elephant's-head pommel.

Elephant-head pommel

Finely etched blade

A close view of the miniature portrait of Josephine, who came to be known as Queen Josefina in Sweden. The artistry is exquisite.

Masterful work in gold by French jewelers

Miniature portraits on the guard

COMMEMORATIVE DRESS SWORD

An extravagantly decorated sword made in 1873 to commemorate the 50th anniversary of the wedding of Josephine of Leuchtenberg and Oscar I of Sweden. The metalwork, inlay, and portraiture were all done by the famed luxury arms manufacturer Fauré Le Page of Paris.

Hunting Swords

Swords have long been used for hunting—in Europe, most especially for hunting wild boar, which was considered a test of courage. As hunting increasingly became the preserve of the aristocracy, hunting swords became treasured items, often given as gifts among friends or allies, and usually conforming to an aesthetic of the chase. Horn grips and decorative motifs of deer, hounds, and wild boar were common.

Designed to administer the final, killing blow to boar or other prey, hunting swords usually had straight, acute, single-edged blades no more than two feet long. Though effective, they were really more about the pastoral fantasy of life in the countryside, away from the intrigues of politics and court life. Modern hunting knives, which often retain such features as horn handles, recall these more aristocratic—and deadly—blades.

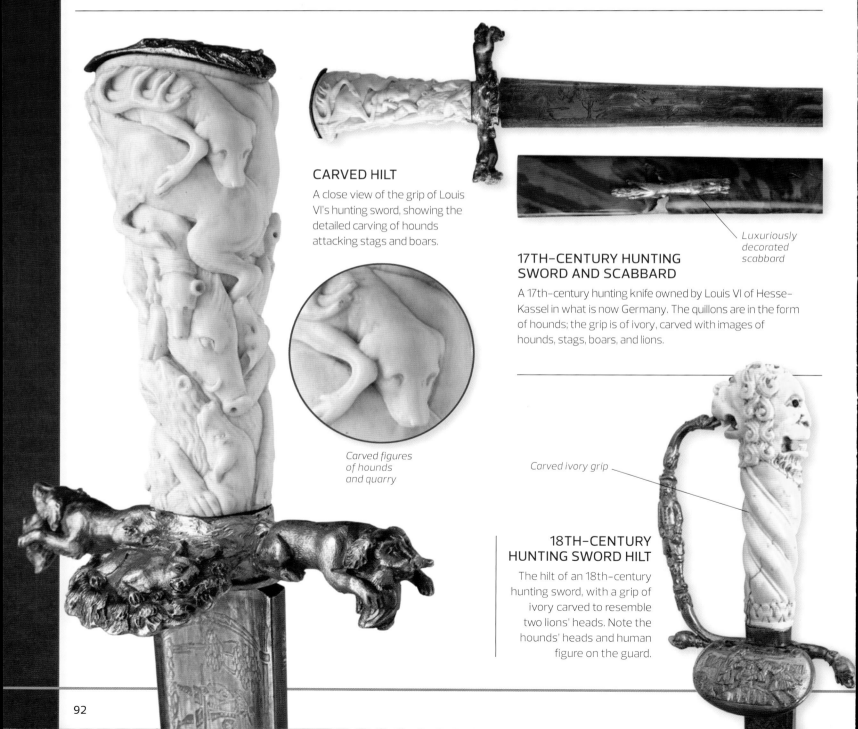

CARVED HILT

A close view of the grip of Louis VI's hunting sword, showing the detailed carving of hounds attacking stags and boars.

Carved figures of hounds and quarry

Luxuriously decorated scabbard

17TH-CENTURY HUNTING SWORD AND SCABBARD

A 17th-century hunting knife owned by Louis VI of Hesse-Kassel in what is now Germany. The quillons are in the form of hounds; the grip is of ivory, carved with images of hounds, stags, boars, and lions.

Carved ivory grip

18TH-CENTURY HUNTING SWORD HILT

The hilt of an 18th-century hunting sword, with a grip of ivory carved to resemble two lions' heads. Note the hounds' heads and human figure on the guard.

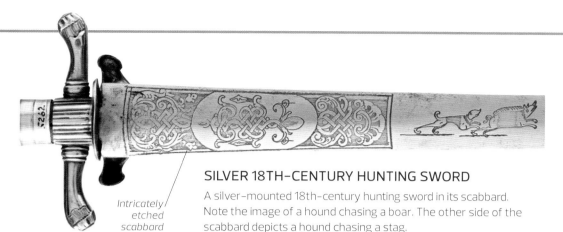

Image of a hound chasing a boar

SILVER 18TH-CENTURY HUNTING SWORD

A silver-mounted 18th-century hunting sword in its scabbard. Note the image of a hound chasing a boar. The other side of the scabbard depicts a hound chasing a stag.

Intricately etched scabbard

18TH-CENTURY STEEL-HANDLED HUNTING SWORD

The carved and gilded hilt of a late 17th-century hunting sword. The decoration depicts classical figures and hunting scenes, in keeping with the pastoral traditions of hunting and country life.

Classical motifs

Scabbard

Fine silver openwork

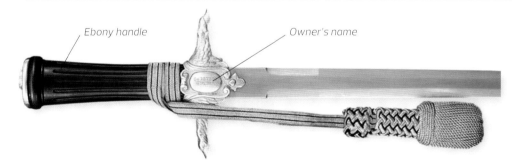

Ebony handle

Owner's name

19TH-CENTURY HUNTING SWORD

A late 19th-century hunting sword with an ebony handle and an elegant rendering of hounds' heads on the quillons. The quillon block is engraved with the owner's name.

Decorative tassel

Grip made of antler

KAISER WILHELM'S HUNTING SWORD

A hunting sword that belonged to Kaiser Wilhelm II, Emperor of Germany from 1888 to 1918. It has a rustic horn grip and relatively simple quillons, along with the image of a boar on its small guard.

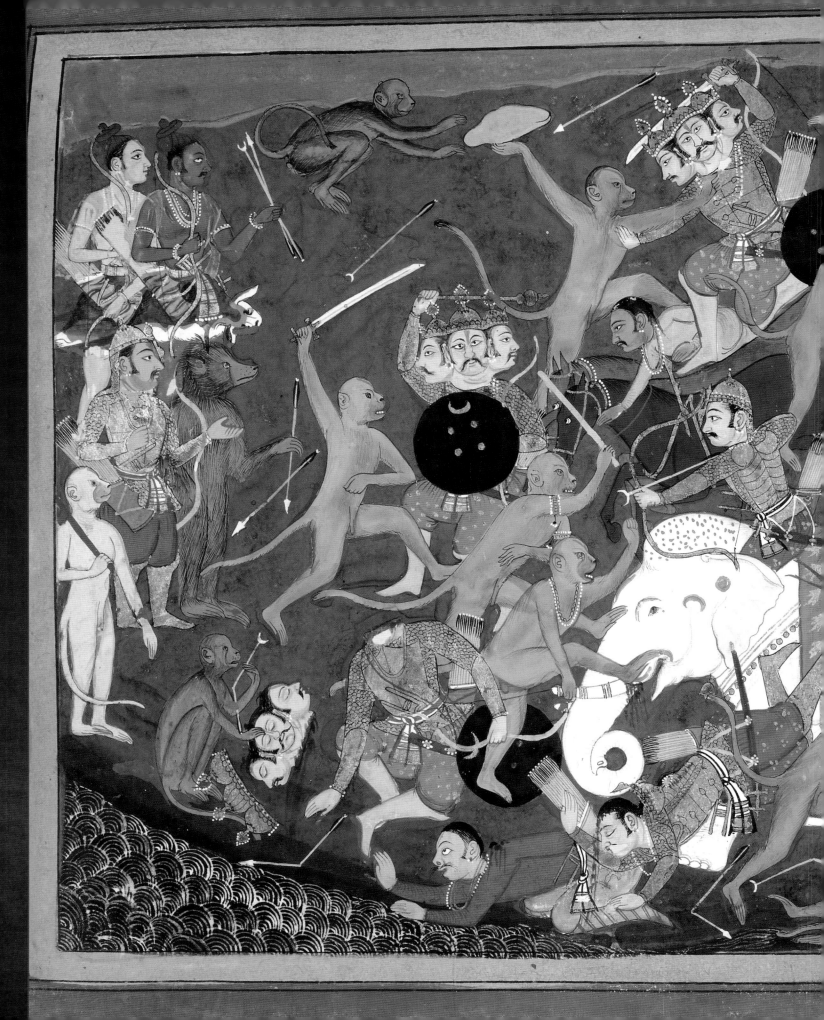

Islamic Weapons

The Artistry of the Islamic Sword

To many Westerners, Islamic swords, especially those that fall under the broad category of scimitars, are icons of an imaginary Orient, conjuring images from *The Thousand and One Nights.* But it is worth remembering that the national flag of Saudi Arabia, home to Mecca and Medina, features two prominent motifs: a calligraphic text of the *shahāda*—the Muslim declaration of faith in the one God and in Mohammed as His Prophet—and a *saif,* an Arabian sword recalling the one wielded by the Prophet himself. As in other civilizations, the sword is both a weapon and a carrier of values, a symbol of tradition and an expression of devotion. And whether they come from as far west as Spain or as far east as India, classic Islamic swords are also exquisite works of art and craftsmanship.

A 17TH-CENTURY narrative depiction of the Battle of Lanka, a key episode in the great Hindu epic the Ramayana. Rama's army of monkeys, led by Hanuman, the Monkey King, subdues a legion of demons under Trisiras. In the lower left corner, Hanuman sits with Trisiras's three severed heads. Rama, serenely detached, surveys the battle from the upper left of the painting.

Sasanian and Persian Swords

Between about 225 and 650 CE, before Persia came under the widening influence of Islam, it was the center of one of the great civilizations of the era: the Sasanian, or Sasanid, Empire. Extending from Pakistan through Egypt at its height, the Sasanian Empire would serve as a model, both administratively and culturally, for the Islamic Caliphates that would follow.

The Sasanian traditions of both art and war were highly developed, and they, too, were passed on to the Islamic civilizations that inherited the former Sasanian lands. The evolution of the Islamic sword begins here, with the straight blades of pre-Islamic Persia.

7TH–CENTURY IVORY IMAGE OF SASANIAN KING

A 7th-century Sasanian ivory carving of a king. The straight sword in his hands is clearly a symbol of power.

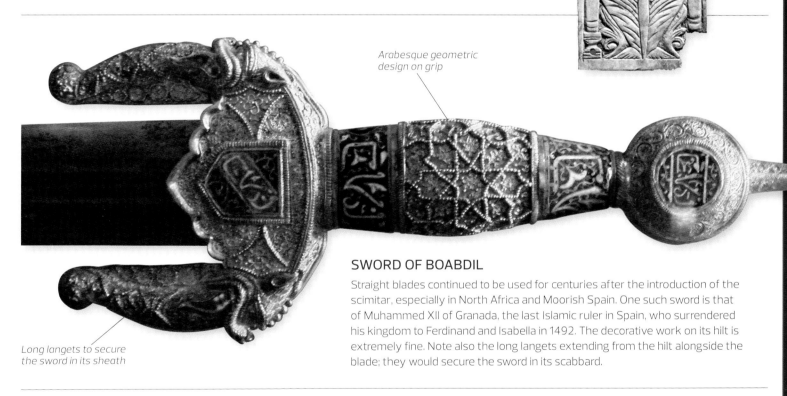

Arabesque geometric design on grip

Long langets to secure the sword in its sheath

SWORD OF BOABDIL

Straight blades continued to be used for centuries after the introduction of the scimitar, especially in North Africa and Moorish Spain. One such sword is that of Muhammed XII of Granada, the last Islamic ruler in Spain, who surrendered his kingdom to Ferdinand and Isabella in 1492. The decorative work on its hilt is extremely fine. Note also the long langets extending from the hilt alongside the blade; they would secure the sword in its scabbard.

7TH–CENTURY SASANIAN GOLD HILTWORK

The elaborate decorative gold used to adorn a 7th-century Sasanian hilt and scabbard. Note how the designs are all abstract, anticipating the intricate patterns of later Islamic art and design.

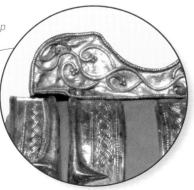

Long, finely decorated grip

Ornamental scabbard bands

Persian Swords

Though many Islamic swords, including perhaps most of those used against the early Crusaders, retained straight blades, by the end of the 8th century Persian blades had taken on a pronounced curve, intended primarily to facilitate their use on horseback. The new form of sword was adopted, and adapted, from the weapons of Turkic horsemen from Central Asia and cavalry sabres from Byzantium. This was the origin of the scimitar, in all its variations.

The word "scimitar" comes from the Persian *shamshir*, meaning "paw claw"—an allusion that probably refers to the blade's sharpness and to its curved claw-like shape. Over the next few centuries, the scimitar's shape would evolve; one especially popular form would be the Turkish *kilij* style, in which the blade narrows before deepening as it curves toward the point.

CLASSIC PERSIAN SCIMITAR

A classic Persian scimitar with elements of the *kilij* style. The elegant blade, inlaid in gold with calligraphic text, often from the Koran, is a thing of beauty. Also shown is the scimitar sheathed, with ornate silver décor on the scabbard. Note how the langets of the cross hilt extend over the outside of the scabbard.

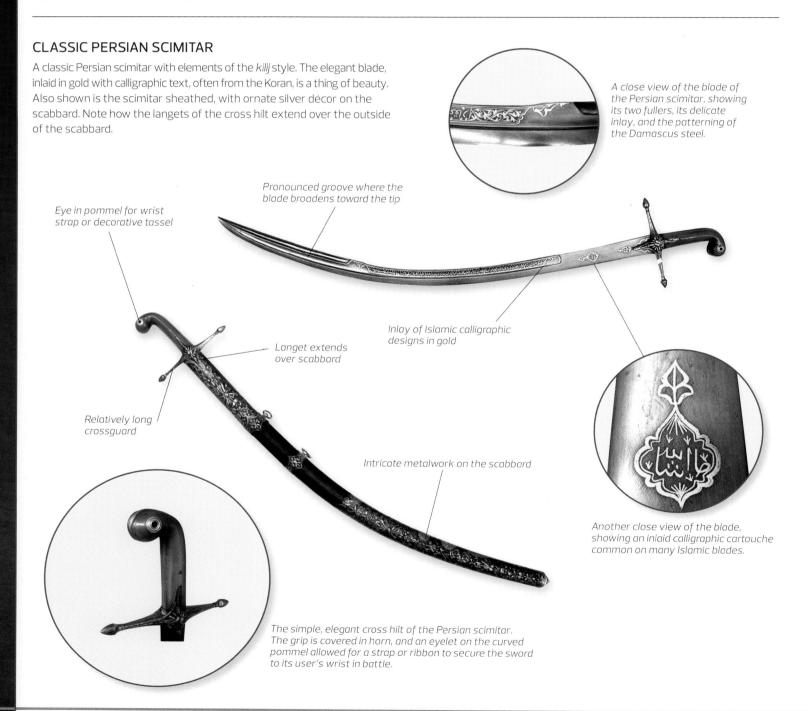

A close view of the blade of the Persian scimitar, showing its two fullers, its delicate inlay, and the patterning of the Damascus steel.

Pronounced groove where the blade broadens toward the tip

Eye in pommel for wrist strap or decorative tassel

Inlay of Islamic calligraphic designs in gold

Langet extends over scabbard

Relatively long crossguard

Intricate metalwork on the scabbard

Another close view of the blade, showing an inlaid calligraphic cartouche common on many Islamic blades.

The simple, elegant cross hilt of the Persian scimitar. The grip is covered in horn, and an eyelet on the curved pommel allowed for a strap or ribbon to secure the sword to its user's wrist in battle.

17TH–CENTURY PERSIAN SHAMSHIR

A Persian *shamshir* with a horn grip and a sweeping curve to its Damascus blade. With the delicate finials on its otherwise unadorned crossguard, the carved but not inlaid designs on its grip, and the elegant profile taper of its blade, this scimitar exemplifies unostentatious elegance.

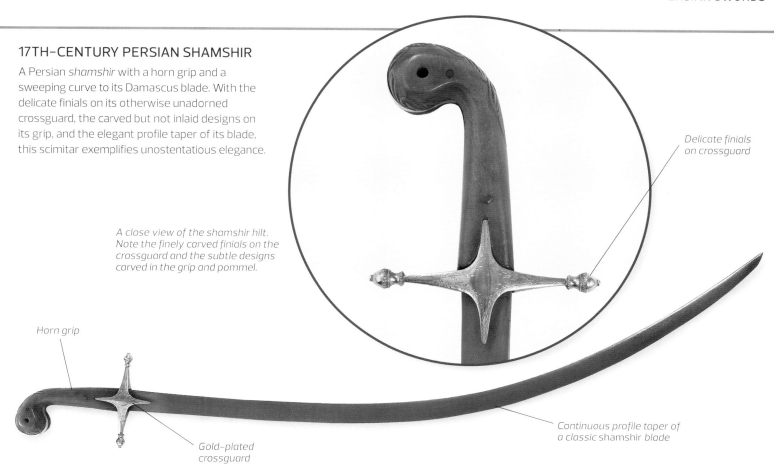

A close view of the shamshir hilt. Note the finely carved finials on the crossguard and the subtle designs carved in the grip and pommel.

Delicate finials on crossguard

Horn grip

Gold–plated crossguard

Continuous profile taper of a classic shamshir *blade*

ISLAMIC CALLIGRAPHY

Islamic culture has produced one of the world's greatest traditions of calligraphy—only those of China and Japan rival it. Partly because Arabic itself was the chief means of preserving and transmitting the Koran, and also because Islam discourages the use of figurative art in sacred spaces, calligraphy became the most esteemed art form of the Islamic world. Though nearly all Islamic calligraphy is in Arabic, a vast range of styles developed from North Africa to India. Abstract compositions of Arabic letters, often framed in cartouches or embedded in geometrical designs, became prominent decorative motifs, used on items ranging from simple boxes to sword blades to royal palaces. The calligraphic cartouches and other inscriptions on Islamic blades may quote Koranic passages, the *shahāda* or Muslim declaration of faith, the name of a sword's owner or maker, or even love poetry. The image shown here is an example of the beauty and dynamism of Islamic calligraphy from the 17th-century Wazir Khan Mosque, built during the reign of Shah Jahan, who also erected the Taj Mahal. The script in the classical Thuluth style, includes the *Basmalah*, which opens every chapter of the Koran: "In the Name of God, the Compassionate, the Merciful."

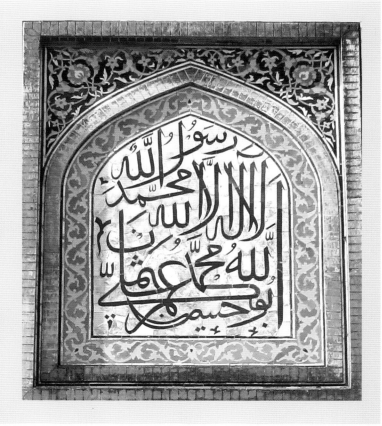

CONSTRUCTION OF THE ISLAMIC SWORD

Islamic swords like the *shamshir* were built quite differently from European weapons of the same period. Islamic blades usually featured short, broad tangs, which were fixed to their hilts with rivets or even adhesives—a surprisingly sturdy method of construction. Also, the swords were balanced differently to European blades; Islamic pommels are not used to counterweight the blade and adjust the sword's center of gravity, but to serve as functional and decorative caps for the grip. This design added force to slashing blows, but also required considerable strength and skill to wield in a melee, especially on foot.

Dating Islamic swords is notoriously difficult, as trusted blades were often remounted over time, and many were well cared for over centuries. Fortunately, quite a few blades are signed and dated by their makers—a feature that allows for some sense of the journey the sword took across generations of ownership.

JEWELED PERSIAN SHAMSHIR

A classic Persian *shamshir* with a richly jeweled hilt. Note the gradual, graceful curve of the blade.

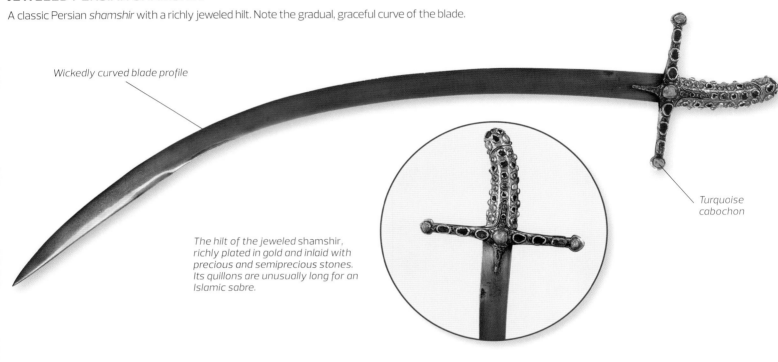

Wickedly curved blade profile

Turquoise cabochon

The hilt of the jeweled shamshir, *richly plated in gold and inlaid with precious and semiprecious stones. Its quillons are unusually long for an Islamic sabre.*

Gold inlay on blade

Ornate lion's head pommel in gold vermeil

15TH/16TH–CENTURY PERSIAN SCIMITAR

A 15th-century Persian scimitar blade mounted to a 16th-century hilt in the form of an elaborate lion's head. Such remounting of blades was very common.

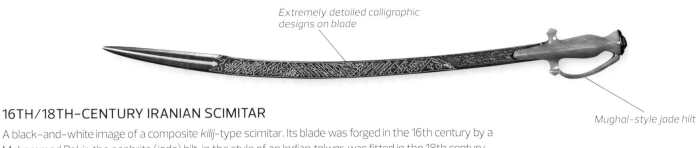

Extremely detailed calligraphic designs on blade

Mughal-style jade hilt

16TH/18TH-CENTURY IRANIAN SCIMITAR

A black-and-white image of a composite *kilij*-type scimitar. Its blade was forged in the 16th century by a Muhammed Bakir; the nephrite (jade) hilt, in the style of an Indian *talwar*, was fitted in the 18th century.

17TH-CENTURY PERSIAN SHAMSHIR

Another classic Persian *shamshir* of the traditional type. Its blade, unlike those of *kilij*-type swords, tapers continuously to a spear point.

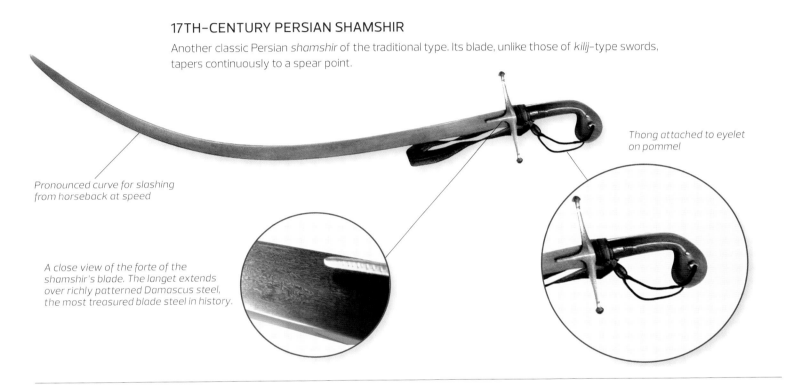

Thong attached to eyelet on pommel

Pronounced curve for slashing from horseback at speed

A close view of the forte of the shamshir's blade. The langet extends over richly patterned Damascus steel, the most treasured blade steel in history.

PERSIAN SHAMSHIR

A superb Persian shamshir with a classic blade of continuous taper. Both the hilt and the scabbard are richly worked, and the blade is beautifully inlaid.

Intricate inlay work on blade

Decorative tassel for formal occasions

Jeweled scabbard

Two Magnificent Persian Swords

The most treasured Persian swords were, naturally, those possessed by rulers and military leaders. Many were used as ceremonial swords to honor extraordinary accomplishments or signify rank, and some found their way into Western collections. Some Islamic blades, usually fitted with Western hilts, featured in the previous chapter. Here are two extraordinary Persian swords that now reside in Western collections.

The first is a scimitar owned by Abbas the Great of Persia (1571–1629), considered the greatest ruler of the Safavid dynasty. The sword was presented by the Ottoman government to Empress Catherine the Great of Russia (1729–1796), and remained in the treasury of the Russian tsars until the 1917 Revolution, after which it vanished before turning up after World War II and being purchased by an American collector. The other scimitar, richly appointed if not as spectacular as that of Abbas the Great, became a coronation sword of Swedish kings.

CLASSIC HILT
The scimitar of Abbas the Great has a classic shamshir hilt, but it is inlaid with diamonds in a pattern surrounding a large ruby.

THE SWORD OF ABBAS THE GREAT
The magnificent sword of Abbas the Great and its matching scabbard, both inlaid with scores of precious stones. The blade is of classic *shamshir* form, with a continuous taper.

JEWELED POMMEL
The pommel of the sword of Abbas ends in a polished emerald that provides a striking contrast to the rubies that feature elsewhere on the sword and scabbard.

MAGNIFICENT SCABBARD
As the most oft-seen part of a sword equipage, the scabbard was an ideal surface for decorative work. Here the top of the scabbard of Abbas's scimitar is inlaid with three large rubies and dozens of diamonds.

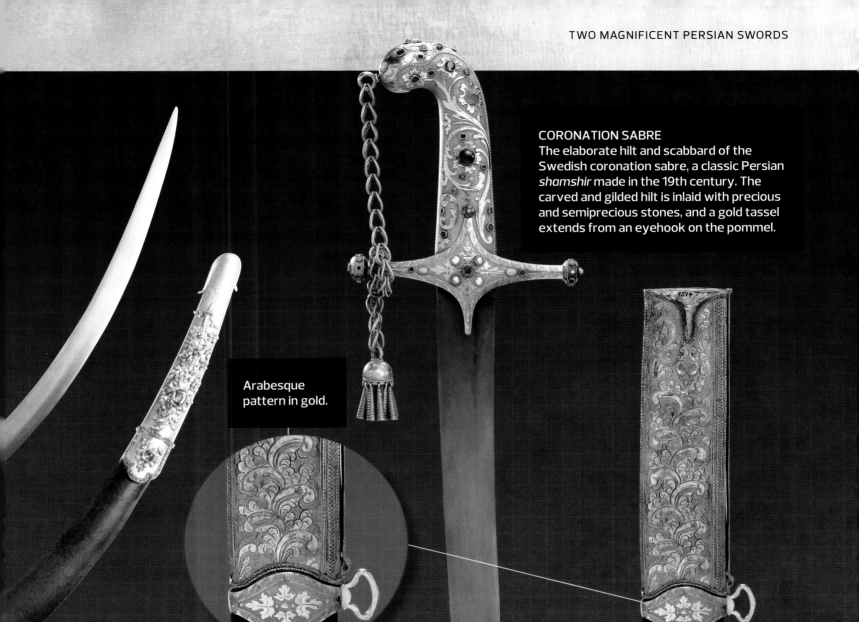

CORONATION SABRE
The elaborate hilt and scabbard of the Swedish coronation sabre, a classic Persian *shamshir* made in the 19th century. The carved and gilded hilt is inlaid with precious and semiprecious stones, and a gold tassel extends from an eyehook on the pommel.

Arabesque pattern in gold.

ABBAS THE GREAT

Abbas I, known as Abbas the Great, Shah (King) of Persia from 1587 until his death in 1629, is considered the greatest ruler of the Safavid dynasty, which ruled Persia from 1501 until 1722. Abbas's reign proved something of a golden age. Though he came to the throne at only 16 years old, he quickly and decisively took control of the powerful military, and then set about patiently expanding his kingdom. In 1598, he moved his capital to the city of Isfahan, which he ordered reorganized and beautified such that it became, and remains, one of the world's most beautiful cities. Under Abbas's rule, Persian art enjoyed a spectacular flowering: painting, ceramics, and textile arts achieved unprecedented splendor. His magnificent *shamshir* only passed to the Ottoman Turks after the fall of the Safavid dynasty a century after his death.

Swords of the Ottoman Empire

The scimitar found its most forceful expression in the weapons of the Ottoman Empire. By the end of the 15th century, the Ottoman Turks had secured control of much of the Middle East, including Egypt—and had absorbed the martial traditions of the Mamelukes, that nation's warrior caste. Adapting what became known in the West as the Mameluke sword, the Ottomans broadened it toward the point, giving it more heft and a balance point closer to the blade tip. The resulting sword was the *kilij*.

In the 16th century, Ottoman swords began to become lighter and their blades shorter, but they remained as effective as they were elegant. Though in later swords the Islamic tradition of inlaid inscriptions began to fade, many Turkish blades have beautiful calligraphic inlays, often establishing ownership or manufacture and including poems as well as Koranic passages.

16TH–CENTURY TURKISH KILIJ

A 16th-century Ottoman *kilij*, with a jeweled hilt and relatively light blade with a pronounced curve.

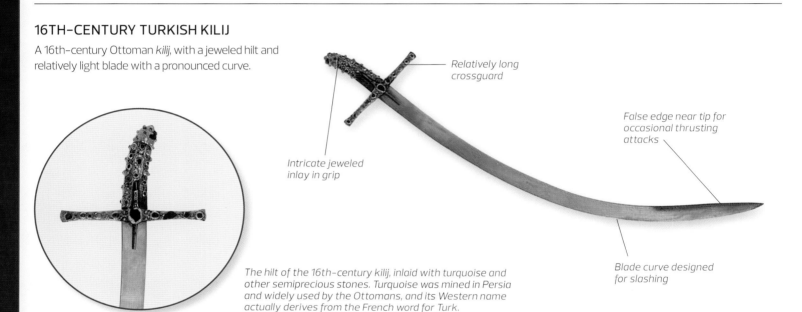

Relatively long crossguard

False edge near tip for occasional thrusting attacks

Intricate jeweled inlay in grip

Blade curve designed for slashing

The hilt of the 16th-century kilij, inlaid with turquoise and other semiprecious stones. Turquoise was mined in Persia and widely used by the Ottomans, and its Western name actually derives from the French word for Turk.

17TH–CENTURY PERSIAN-TURKISH KILIJ

A Persian *kilij* blade remounted on a Turkish hilt, from the 17th century. Note the inlay work on the blade and the decorative embellishments on the scabbard.

A closer view of the hilt and scabbard. The openwork on the grip reveals the horn beneath the detailed overlay of gold and semiprecious stones.

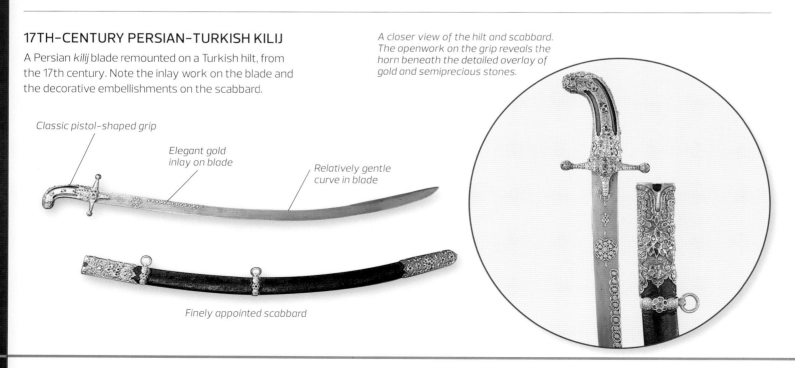

Classic pistol-shaped grip

Elegant gold inlay on blade

Relatively gentle curve in blade

Finely appointed scabbard

OTTOMAN KILIJ

A supremely elegant Ottoman *kilij*, with silver and gold inlay work but little of the dense adornment that can sometimes make such swords look a bit overdone.

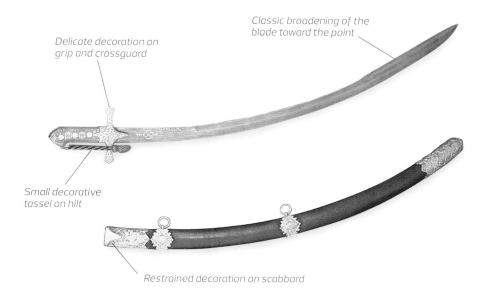

Classic broadening of the blade toward the point

Delicate decoration on grip and crossguard

Small decorative tassel on hilt

Restrained decoration on scabbard

A close view of the hilt. The grip is made of agate, inlaid with gold in cartouches and other patterns that parallel the blade. In its reserved elegance, this hilt is extraordinarily refined.

17TH-CENTURY OTTOMAN SCIMITARS

Three extravagantly mounted Turkish scimitars. Such rich ornamentation reflected the splendor of the Ottoman court.

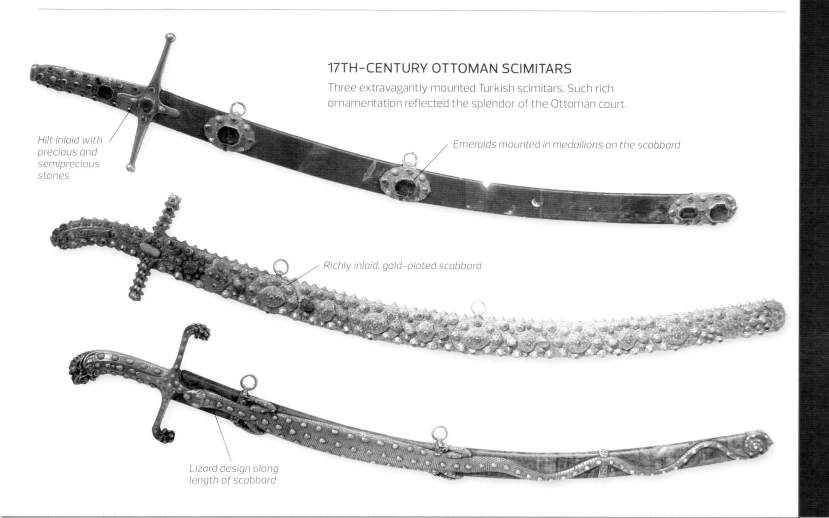

Hilt inlaid with precious and semiprecious stones

Emeralds mounted in medallions on the scabbard

Richly inlaid, gold-plated scabbard

Lizard design along length of scabbard

KILIJ WITH NEPHRITE HILT

An Ottoman scimitar with a jade hilt and the classic blade profile of a *kilij*.

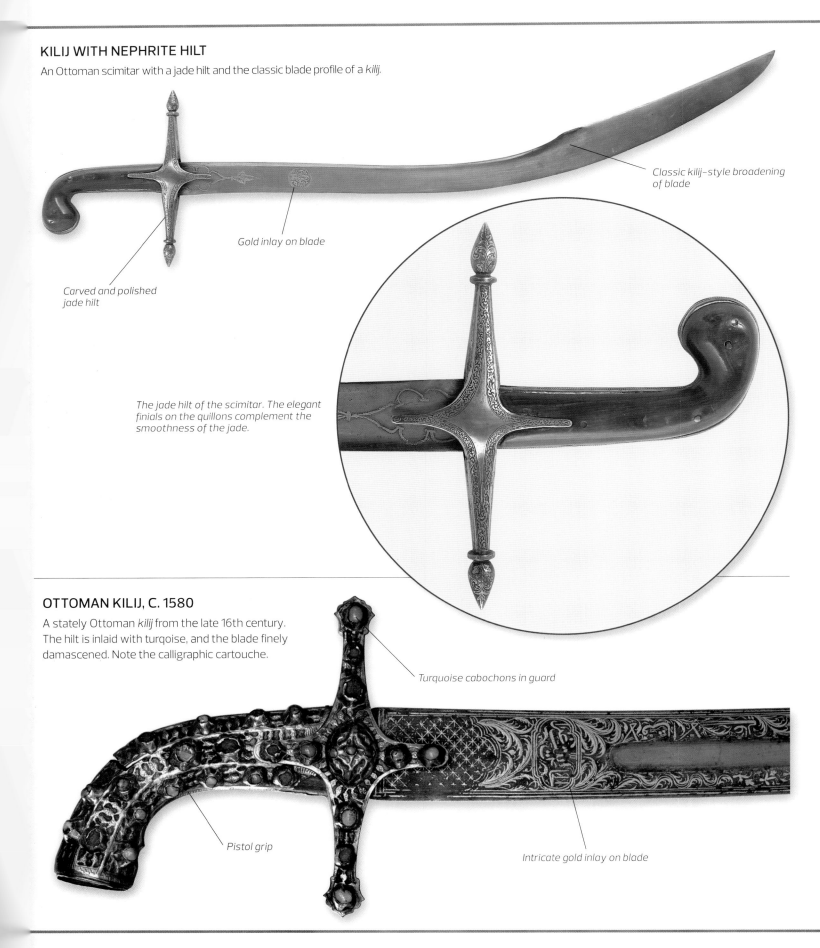

Classic kilij–style broadening of blade

Gold inlay on blade

Carved and polished jade hilt

The jade hilt of the scimitar. The elegant finials on the quillons complement the smoothness of the jade.

OTTOMAN KILIJ, C. 1580

A stately Ottoman *kilij* from the late 16th century. The hilt is inlaid with turqoise, and the blade finely damascened. Note the calligraphic cartouche.

Turquoise cabochons in guard

Pistol grip

Intricate gold inlay on blade

THE MAMELUKES

The Mamelukes, or Mamluks, were some of the most feared and respected warriors in history. They began in the 9th century as slaves, brought from outside the Baghdad Caliphate to be trained as a military elite without any ties to local tribes or chiefs who might conspire against the Caliph. Over the centuries, they evolved into a caste of their own, achieving a social rank above ordinary citizens and even, in places such as Egypt and Syria, eventually gaining supreme power. It was the Mamelukes who ultimately fended off both the Crusaders and the Mongols, and they remained a crucial part of many Islamic societies, including that of the Ottoman Turks, until the 19th century.

As a rule, Mamelukes were bought as slaves when young, and they were educated to become Muslim warriors, learning both Arabic and the arts of war. Their training completed, they were technically no longer slaves but usually remained attached to their original purchasers, or patrons, and lived in garrisons. Mamelukes followed an Islamic form of the chivalric code, and were mostly revered as defenders of Islam by their fellow citizens.

An 1825 Greek lithograph of a Turkish Mameluke, his left hand on the scabbard of an impressive scimitar. The Ottomans absorbed the Egyptian tradition of the Mamelukes.

19TH-CENTURY INDO-OTTOMAN *SHAMSHIR*

The scimitar of Mehmed Ali Pasha (1827–1878), a German who converted to Islam and became a formidable military leader for the Ottoman Empire, fighting in the Crimean War. The sword's hilt is jade, and its blade is damascened in pure gold.

Carved jade hilt

Imperially decorated scabbard

Regal gold inlay in blade

18TH-CENTURY KILIJ

A refined 18th-century Ottoman *kilij* with an ivory grip and Damascus blade. The calligraphic cartouche on the blade identifies its maker: Ali ibn Abi Talib.

Decorative tassel

Cartouche inlaid in blade

The scimitar of Ali ibn Abi Talib sheathed. Its scabbard, like portions of its hilt, is of elegantly worked silver.

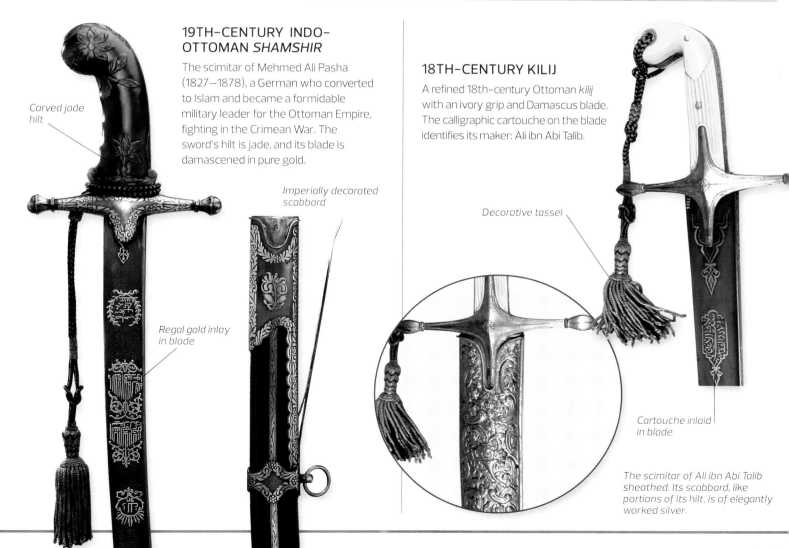

Other Ottoman Blades

Though the scimitar became the iconic sword of the Ottoman Empire, it was not the only form of blade used by Turkish forces. Different blade profiles, drawn from a range of traditions incorporated into Ottoman culture, played valuable roles on the battlefield and as ceremonial dress.

The most famous of these other swords was the *yataghan*, a short sword with a slight inward curve and the reliable combination of a relatively pliant spine and a hard,

durable edge. Janissaries, the Ottoman Empire's elite infantry, favored the *yataghan* for its lightness and its effectiveness in close combat. Ottoman troops also used European-style thrusting swords with stiff blades, called "armor knitters," to exploit gaps in the heavy armor of their enemies. Both kinds of swords were found with simple, battle-ready construction and ornately decorated dress or ceremonial forms.

TWO TURKISH YATAGHAN

Two Turkish *yataghan* from the 18th and 19th centuries. Their grips, typical of *yataghans*, are made of two "eared" grip plaques, of ivory in these exampes, riveted together through the tang.

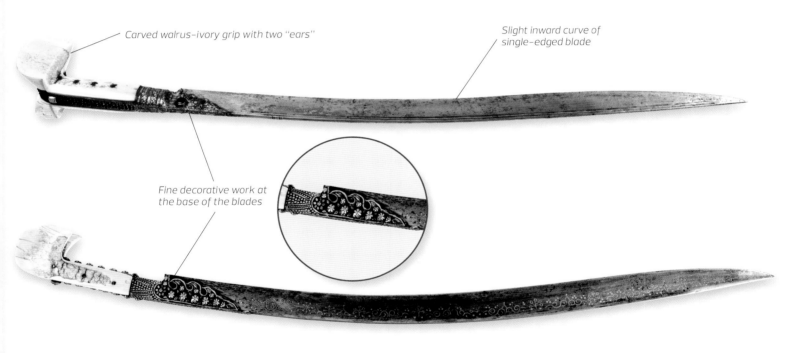

Carved walrus-ivory grip with two "ears"

Slight inward curve of single-edged blade

Fine decorative work at the base of the blades

OTTOMAN YATAGHAN

A beautifully made and decorated Ottoman yataghan from the late 18th century. Both the hilt and the scabbard are adorned in meticulously worked silver and inlays, clearly marking this as a dress sword rather than a combat weapon, but the blade is still combat-worthy.

Extraordinarily delicate decorative work on grip and pommel

Carved silver-plated scabbard

Hilt inlaid with semiprecious stones

Finely detailed gold damascene on blade

Exquisite fittings on scabbard

OTTOMAN PALLASCH

An Ottoman *pallasch*—the word was derived from the Turkish *pala*, or straight, to indicate the straight, heavy, single-edged blade. This example is very elegantly made, with a hilt of ivory and a scabbard studded with precious stones. Its magnificently inlaid Damascus blade, double-edged toward the tip, is just shy of two feet long, making this a short sword suited for close combat—if such an expensive blade would ever actually see that sort of rough use. While not the most prominent weapon in the Ottoman armory, the *pallasch* gained great favor in the West, where it became the model for a number of military backswords (single-edged swords with a thick flat edge opposite the cutting edge).

A close view of the pallasch's expertly done intricate inlay, which combines floral motifs with Arabic calligraphy.

17TH-CENTURY TURKISH ARMOR KNITTER

The sheathed hilt of an extravagantly decorated "armor knitter" sword, so named because its acute blade was used for thrusting attacks against the joints and weak points in plate and other heavy armor. The gold- and silver-plated scabbard and hilt are studded with turquoise, jade, and rubies. Though this weapon is clearly not meant for combat, its large pommel and inlaid precious and semiprecious stones are not merely for ornamentation; they also provide a sure grip.

Prominent round pommel

Large cabochons of semiprecious stones

Scabbard studded with turquoise and other stones

Swords of the Mughal Empire

The Mughal Empire, established by the ruler Babur in the 16th century, would include most of the Indian subcontinent until the institution of the British Raj in 1857. The Mughal emperors themselves were of Turko-Mongol background, and generally practiced broad tolerance in religious and cultural matters, though they adopted a Persianized culture themselves. The resulting mélange of Indic and Persian cultures produced some of the most remarkable art and architecture in the world, most famously the Taj Mahal.

The swords of Mughal India were also largely Persian in design, but they developed their own distinct forms. The kind of scimitar that became most identified with the Mughals was the *talwar*, which had a blade with a shallow enough curve to be used for both slashing and thrusting, a prominent disk-shaped pommel, and a balance point closer to the hilt than many Islamic blades. Other forms of sword, some even fantastical, appeared during the Mughal era.

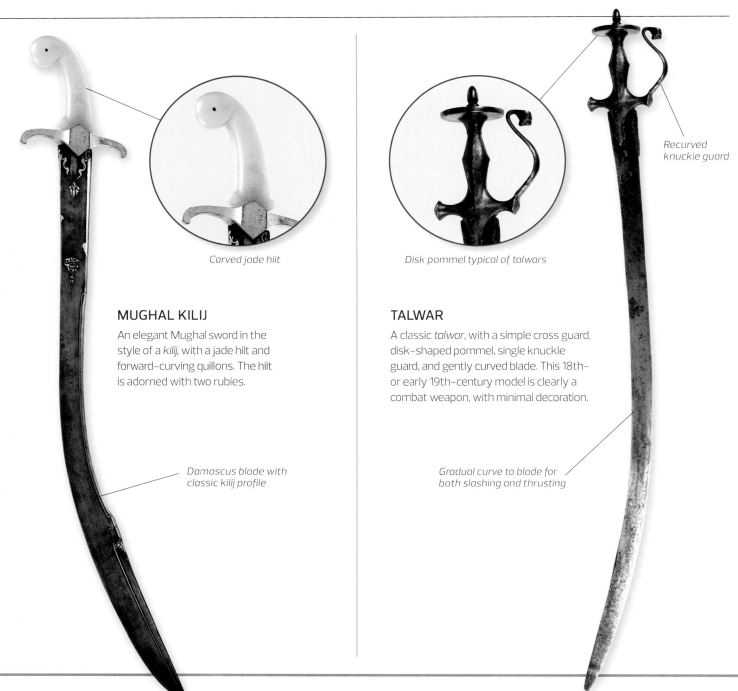

Carved jade hilt

Disk pommel typical of talwars

Recurved knuckle guard

MUGHAL KILIJ

An elegant Mughal sword in the style of a *kilij*, with a jade hilt and forward-curving quillons. The hilt is adorned with two rubies.

Damascus blade with classic kilij profile

TALWAR

A classic *talwar*, with a simple cross guard, disk-shaped pommel, single knuckle guard, and gently curved blade. This 18th- or early 19th-century model is clearly a combat weapon, with minimal decoration.

Gradual curve to blade for both slashing and thrusting

MUGHAL SHAMSHIR

A Mughal *shamshir* of decidedly Persian form, with its scabbard and baldrick. The sword has a grip of ivory and a mostly decorative beaded knuckle guard.

Baldric for secure carrying

The beautiful Damascus steel of the Mughal shamshir. The stylized characters inlaid in the blade are the name of its maker: Sharafollah.

Ivory pistol grip

Beaded knuckle guard

Pronounced, slashing curve in blade

Reinforced scabbard tip

MUGHAL SHAMSHIR HILT

The hilt of the Mughal *shamshir*, with its ivory grip, agate and other beads, and enameled guard.

MUGHAL WARRIORS IN ART

Mughal painting is one of the world's great artistic legacies; along with Mughal architecture, it exemplifies the remarkable merging of Persian and Indic traditions that took place during the Mughal Empire (1526–1857). Most strikingly, a Persian sense of elegance combined with an Indic love of color and descriptive detail. The resulting paintings, generally made for books or albums, are filled with stunningly precise brushwork, and offer a fascinating window on Mughal civilization. Though these paintings depict a wide and fascinating range of people, places, and things, many depict warriors, either as set portraits or as lively and sometimes even graphic images of training and combat. The fencing traditions of the Indian subcontinent differ from most Western forms of swordplay in that, rather than emphasize economy of movement, they encourage acrobatic agility and elaborate feints. Such moves can be found illustrated in the pages of Mughal books. The illustration shown here is a 17th-century Mughal image of two warriors in combat. Both carry swords that resemble *talwars*, with gently curved blades but without the typical knuckle guard. Note the broken blade of the fallen warrior's sword, and the clear advantage a curved blade affords to the mounted warrior, who is also equipped with a bow and arrows.

Other Islamic Weapons

Though the sword is the weapon most associated with Islamic martial traditions, a range of weapons was used by the warriors of the various Muslim states and empires. Maces (largely similar to those found elsewhere in Europe and Asia) were often used as symbols of authority, and axes and war-hammers were used effectively against heavily armored foes. Many of these weapons displayed a level of craftsmanship and decorative richness nearly equal to that of prized scimitars.

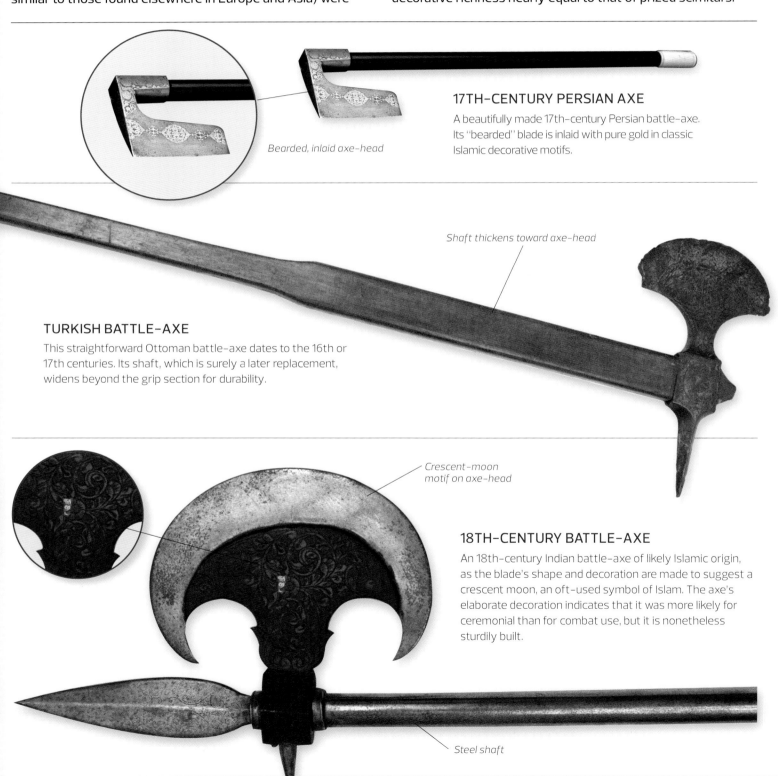

Bearded, inlaid axe-head

17TH-CENTURY PERSIAN AXE

A beautifully made 17th-century Persian battle-axe. Its "bearded" blade is inlaid with pure gold in classic Islamic decorative motifs.

Shaft thickens toward axe-head

TURKISH BATTLE-AXE

This straightforward Ottoman battle-axe dates to the 16th or 17th centuries. Its shaft, which is surely a later replacement, widens beyond the grip section for durability.

Crescent-moon motif on axe-head

18TH-CENTURY BATTLE-AXE

An 18th-century Indian battle-axe of likely Islamic origin, as the blade's shape and decoration are made to suggest a crescent moon, an oft-used symbol of Islam. The axe's elaborate decoration indicates that it was more likely for ceremonial than for combat use, but it is nonetheless sturdily built.

Steel shaft

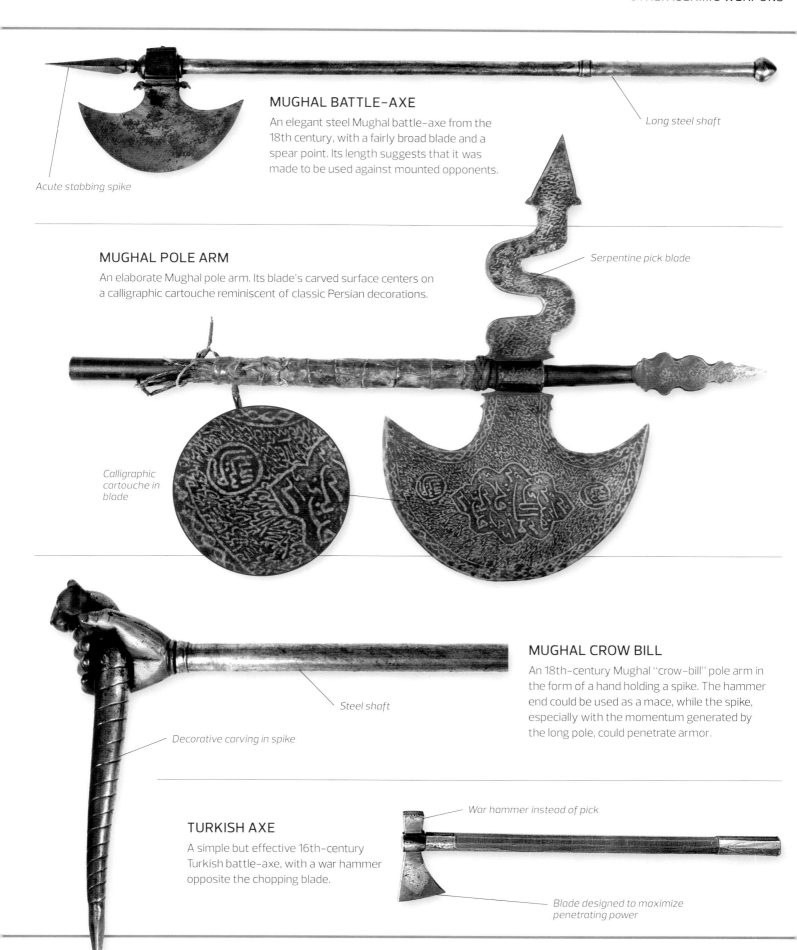

Long steel shaft

MUGHAL BATTLE-AXE

An elegant steel Mughal battle-axe from the 18th century, with a fairly broad blade and a spear point. Its length suggests that it was made to be used against mounted opponents.

Acute stabbing spike

MUGHAL POLE ARM

An elaborate Mughal pole arm. Its blade's carved surface centers on a calligraphic cartouche reminiscent of classic Persian decorations.

Serpentine pick blade

Calligraphic cartouche in blade

MUGHAL CROW BILL

An 18th-century Mughal "crow-bill" pole arm in the form of a hand holding a spike. The hammer end could be used as a mace, while the spike, especially with the momentum generated by the long pole, could penetrate armor.

Steel shaft

Decorative carving in spike

War hammer instead of pick

TURKISH AXE

A simple but effective 16th-century Turkish battle-axe, with a war hammer opposite the chopping blade.

Blade designed to maximize penetrating power

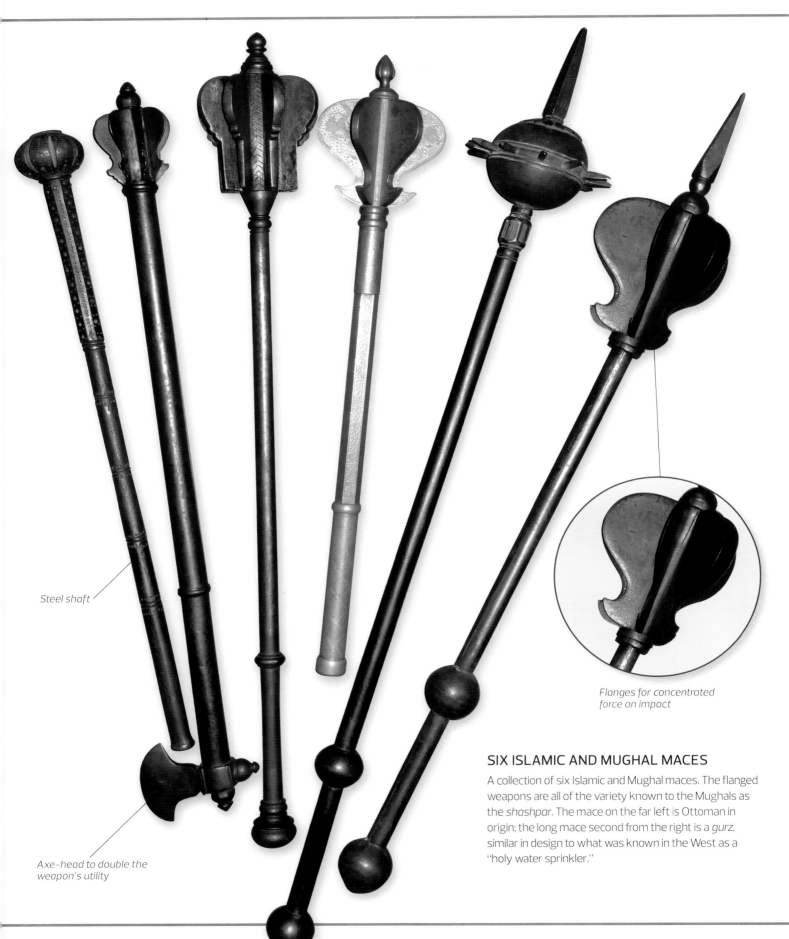

Steel shaft

Axe-head to double the
weapon's utility

Flanges for concentrated
force on impact

SIX ISLAMIC AND MUGHAL MACES

A collection of six Islamic and Mughal maces. The flanged
weapons are all of the variety known to the Mughals as
the *shashpar*. The mace on the far left is Ottoman in
origin; the long mace second from the right is a *gurz*,
similar in design to what was known in the West as a
"holy water sprinkler."

TABAR-SHASHPAR

Relatively small mace head

An 18th-century *tabar-shashpar* (axe-mace) from the Deccan. Mughal in style, it is a rare example of a two-ended, dual-purpose weapon.

SHASHPAR

Decorative finial

A classic *shashpar*, or flanged mace, with eight flanges. Note how the shaft is constructed to secure its user's grip while swinging the weapon in the heat of battle.

Ring on shaft to mark grip section

MUGHAL WAR HAMMER

A Mughal war hammer, with a spike crafted to resemble an antelope horn. The grooves in the horn are gold-filled.

Replacement wooden shaft

Gold inlay in "horn" pick

Coins for added damage

ILLUSTRATION OF OTTOMAN TROOPS

A 1568 Hungarian illustration of Ottoman troops on horseback. One holds a Western-style lance; the warrior on the far left wields a war hammer.

Wooden shaft with woven grip

TURKISH MACE

A rather crude but effective Turkish mace, with a spear point and several weighty coins chained to the head for maximum damage.

Islamic Weapons from Arabia and North Africa

Islam originated in the Arabian Peninsula, and in short order it spread through North Africa. The weapons of both regions have distinctive qualities. The Arabian *saif*, with its distinctively large and secure hilt, acutely curved blade, and viciously sharp tip spawned similar weapons across the Sahara and Mediterranean coast to Morocco and Moorish Spain. The fiercely independent tribes of the Sahara and Sahel, such as the Touareg, had blades of their own that drew on both Arabian and Sub–Saharan African influences.

BARBARY PIRATE SCIMITAR

A *kilij*-type scimitar taken from a Barbary Pirate as a trophy by a British Marine, probably during the Second Barbary War in 1815.

Functional, relatively unadorned sheath

Chain–link knuckle guard

NIMCHA

This North African *nimcha* is similar to a classic Arabian *saif*. Both the large, distinct hilt and acute, curving blade are common to both weapons.

Overbuilt, secure hilt

Geometric designs on scabbard

KASKARA

A Sudanese *kaskara* and scabbard. The *kaskara*, with its cross hilt and broad slashing blade with little taper, was the essential weapon of Sudanese warriors, and was worn slung across the back. Similar weapons, such as the *takouba* of the warlike Tuareg tribes, were widely used in North Africa through the 19th century, and are often carried today.

PORTRAIT OF MOORISH AMBASSADOR TO ELIZABETH I

A portrait from 1600 of Abd el-Ouahed ben Messaoud ben Mohammed Anoun, who served as Moorish Ambassador late in the reign of Queen Elizabeth I. His sword has the hilt of an Arabian *saif* and a blade with little curvature. Note how the baldrick from which the sword hangs is itself used as a decorative surface.

"Ears" and spur on pommel

Hardwood grip inlaid with emeralds

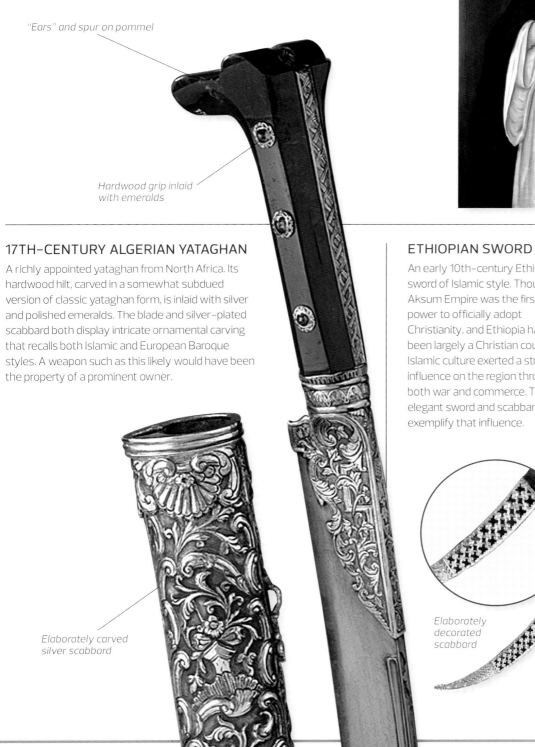

17TH–CENTURY ALGERIAN YATAGHAN

A richly appointed yataghan from North Africa. Its hardwood hilt, carved in a somewhat subdued version of classic yataghan form, is inlaid with silver and polished emeralds. The blade and silver–plated scabbard both display intricate ornamental carving that recalls both Islamic and European Baroque styles. A weapon such as this likely would have been the property of a prominent owner.

Elaborately carved silver scabbard

ETHIOPIAN SWORD

An early 10th-century Ethiopian sword of Islamic style. Though the Aksum Empire was the first major power to officially adopt Christianity, and Ethiopia has since been largely a Christian country, Islamic culture exerted a strong influence on the region through both war and commerce. This elegant sword and scabbard exemplify that influence.

Wide pommel for secure grip

Elaborately decorated scabbard

Blade has a moderate curve for both slashing and occasional stabbing

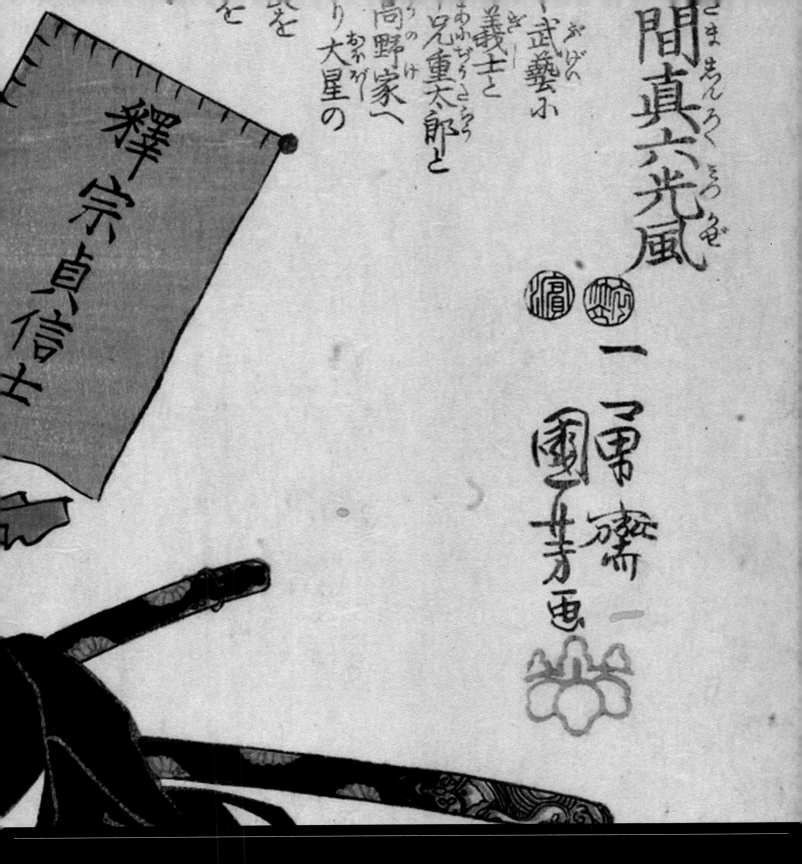

Weapons of the Far East

The Blades of China and Japan

Of all the world's martial traditions, perhaps none have treasured the sword more than those of China and, especially, Japan. In both cultures, the martial arts and their weapons were at once effective tools, markers of social status, and potent symbols of spiritual discipline. Eventually, Japanese swords would achieve the most sublime union of function and form, lethality and beauty, of any bladed weapons.

A 19TH-CENTURY woodblock print showing a samurai poised for battle, a banner attached to his back. The artist has indicated the temper-line of the samurai's *katana*.

Early Chinese Swords

The great East Asian traditions of swordmaking and swordfighting can be traced back to early China. From the Chou Dynasty (1122–770 BCE) onward, Chinese swordsmiths continually refined their blades, both in form and in forging. The Chinese invested their finest swords with extraordinary value; many of the finer blades were given names, and were regarded as beings in their own right.

In the Warring States Period (approximately 475–221 BCE), China was divided among seven major states as well as lesser realms, and nearly constant warfare raged until the triumph and consolidation of the Han Dynasty. Swords from this period, made of both bronze and steel, set the standard form for the straight combat sword of Chinese civilization, the *jian*. Later, during the Han dynasty, Chinese swordsmiths developed the techniques of laminating and differential hardening that would achieve their finest expression in Japan.

WARRING STATES SWORD

A well-preserved sword from the Warring States period, in the classic style of the *jian*, or two-edged straight sword. Note the chevron patterning in the bronze.

Well-preserved, decorated blade

EASTERN ZHOU SWORD

This well-preserved bronze blade from the Warring States period has a clear central ridge. The grip would have been wrapped with silk cord or similar material.

SWORD OF GOUJIAN

The Sword of Goujian, a King of Yue from the Spring and Autumn period (771–403 BCE). Unearthed in 1965, it was found in astoundingly good condition due to the quality of its bronze alloy and the tight seal of its lacquered scabbard. Just under two feet long, it is inscribed with ancient seal script.

BRONZE SWORD, TRIPLE VIEW

A triple view of a typical bronze *jian*, with disk-shaped guard and pommel and finger grooves in the grip.

SUI DYNASTY SWORDS

These slender, single-edged swords from the Sui Dynasty (581–618 CE) are the kind that exerted the greatest influence on Japanese swordmakers, who would eventually make some of the world's finest blades.

Slender, straight blade

Later Chinese Swords

The Chinese sword evolved continuously over the next millennium, as swordsmiths refined their techniques and absorbed outside influences. In the first millennium BCE, Chinese swordmakers took up such practices as using rayskin for secure grips and applying clay coatings during the tempering process to differentially harden blades. From abroad came the Persian hilt, Damascus steel, and fine Japanese blades. During the later Han and Sui Dynasties, single-edged straight blades with chisel-like points that influenced those made in Japan. In the 13th century, after repeated clashes with the Mongols, the *dao*, or curved, single-edged sabre, became an important part of the Chinese armory.

Through it all, the jian remained as the ideal sword. Known as "the gentleman of weapons," it actually evolved into two distinct forms. The first, the *wu jian* or battle sword, kept the heft and sturdiness of the classic straight swords of earlier periods. The second, the "scholar's sword" or *wen jian*, was far lighter and more flexible, and had a rounded point. Used only for self-defense and, later, some martial arts, the scholar's sword was associated with the Chinese literati. Many *wen jian*, like some on these pages, were beautifully mounted and skillfully decorated.

LONG CHINESE SWORD

A scholar's sword with a blade of just over 31 inches, fitted with beautifully made cloisonné enamel mountings. Note how the tip of the sword is slightly rounded rather than acute.

Intricate floral cloisonné on guard

Elaborate cloisonné work

QING DYNASTY WARRIOR WITH DAO

A striking image from the late 18th century of a Qing Dynasty warrior. Though his chief weapon is clearly the bow, he wears a *dao*—a curved, single-edged sabre—at his waist.

CHINESE SABRE

A highly unusual sabre, made in China from the blade of a Japanese sword. The tang of the Japanese blade is still visible above the guard.

A close view of the composite sabre's hilt. The curved guard is carved with a lizard-skin pattern, and the grip is made of ivory carved and dyed red.

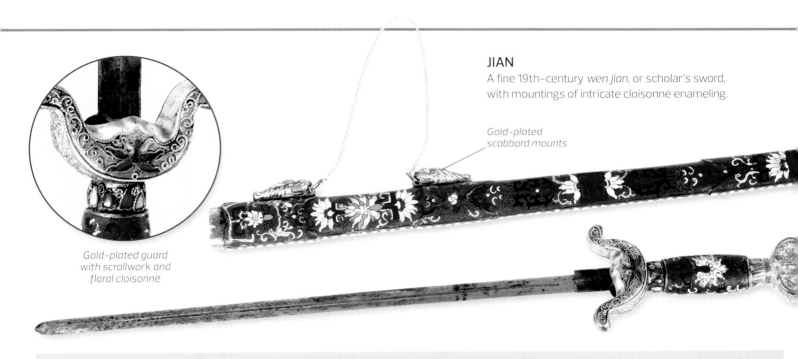

JIAN
A fine 19th-century *wen jian*, or scholar's sword, with mountings of intricate cloisonné enameling.

Gold-plated scabbard mounts

Gold-plated guard with scrollwork and floral cloisonné

THE SCHOLAR'S SWORD: THE SUBTLEST OF BLADES

Thanks to Chinese epic films of recent years, when most Westerners think of a Chinese sword, they tend to envision the *wen jian*. This is actually fitting, as this sword has come to be regarded as the most elegant and exalted sword in Chinese culture. For centuries, officials and aristocrats wore such swords to the imperial court. During the Qing dynasty (1644—1911), the *wen jian* came to be closely associated with the martial art of *Tai Chi Chuan*. The blade of the *wen jian*, too flexible for the hacking and stiff parrying of conventional combat, was perfect for the internal disciplines of *Tai Chi Chuan*, in which one meets hardness with softness, redirects an opponents' force, and uses strikes to transmit vital energy (*chi*) rather than crude physical force. The image shown here depicts a Taoist immortal carrying a scholar's sword across his back.

FANG
An unusual stirrup-hilted, double-edged Chinese sword called a fang. The sharpened hook on the blade is intended for cutting the bridle or reins of an enemy's horse.

Hook blade for cutting horse reins and bridles

Forward-curved guard

Other Chinese Weapons

In the long history of Chinese warfare, soldiers have used a remarkable variety of weapons. Most, however, conform to the essential archetypes that have governed most weapons throughout history: sword, spear, bow, axe, and club. Still, the Chinese brought tremendous artistry and ingenuity to their designs. Here are just a few examples that showcase the beauty and effectiveness of such weapons.

DAGGER-AXE HEAD

The head of a dagger-axe, a pole arm used widely during the Qin dynasty (221–206 BCE). The blade could be used for both thrusting and scything attacks.

Hacking and slashing curve to blade

BRONZE SPEARHEAD

This bronze spearhead from the early Han dynasty (206 BCE–220 CE) is decorated with two curious human figures hanging from the blade.

Gruesome figures hang from blade

CHINESE POLE ARM

A *fu pa*, or "tiger fork" pole arm. Though it is sometimes said to derive from weapons used to fend off tigers, it may be simply a wider, more refined form of the classic Chinese battle lance.

Fork shape for both stabbing and hooking

QI BATTLE-AXE

A very early bronze battle-axe with a circular blade for wide slashing and chopping strikes. The animal ornamenting the haft is probably totemic.

Totemic motif

Circular axe-head

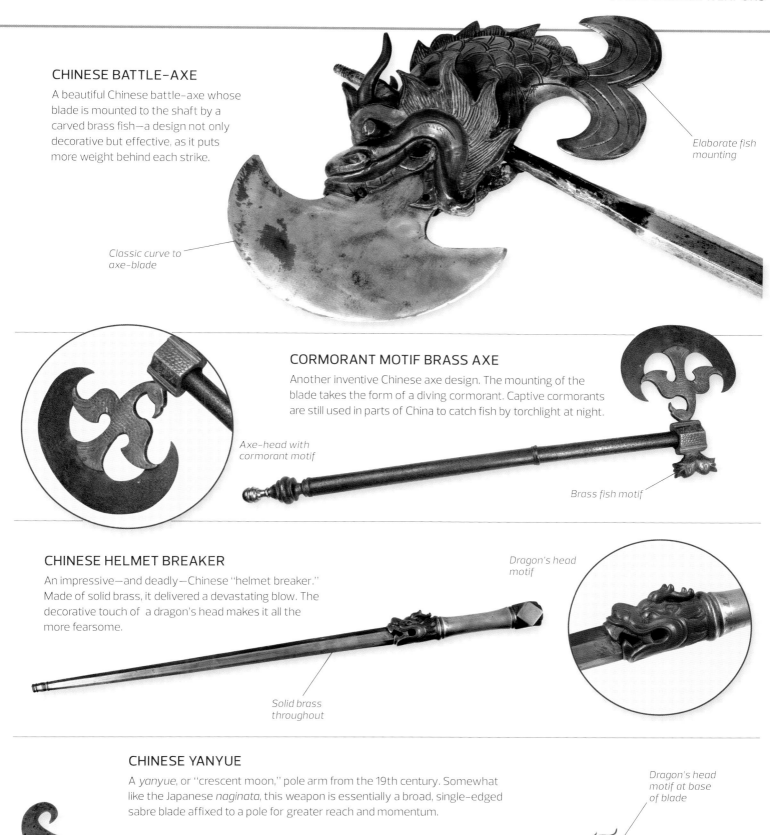

CHINESE BATTLE-AXE

A beautiful Chinese battle-axe whose blade is mounted to the shaft by a carved brass fish—a design not only decorative but effective, as it puts more weight behind each strike.

Elaborate fish mounting

Classic curve to axe-blade

CORMORANT MOTIF BRASS AXE

Another inventive Chinese axe design. The mounting of the blade takes the form of a diving cormorant. Captive cormorants are still used in parts of China to catch fish by torchlight at night.

Axe-head with cormorant motif

Brass fish motif

CHINESE HELMET BREAKER

An impressive—and deadly—Chinese "helmet breaker." Made of solid brass, it delivered a devastating blow. The decorative touch of a dragon's head makes it all the more fearsome.

Dragon's head motif

Solid brass throughout

CHINESE YANYUE

A *yanyue*, or "crescent moon," pole arm from the 19th century. Somewhat like the Japanese *naginata*, this weapon is essentially a broad, single-edged sabre blade affixed to a pole for greater reach and momentum.

Dragon's head motif at base of blade

Japanese Swords: Tachi

In Japan, the sword is one of three items that have always made up the imperial regalia. For millennia, certain swords have been regarded as the earthly residences of divine spirits. Such reverence for the sword led to the most extraordinary traditions of swordmaking and swordsmanship the world has ever seen.

After Chinese techniques of lamination and differential hardening arrived in Japan in the early decades of the Heian period (794—1185), Japanese swordsmiths immediately exercised what has become a hallmark of their civilization: the ability to adopt foreign technologies and transform them into distinctly Japanese traditions. The resulting swords were adapted to the conventions of the Japanese warfare of the time: largely mounted, based on the bow and arrow, and, in keeping with Heian culture, highly aestheticized. Records of

the time refer to a days-long process of polishing blades, to say nothing of forging them.

The longsword of the Heian period, which would with slight variations predominate until the 16th century, was the *tachi*. The *tachi* was a two-handed, single-edged, curved sword, the curve often occurring close to the hilt. It was made of intricately laminated and differentially polished steel, and usually about thirty inches in length. It was worn with the edge down, and often fitted with gorgeous mountings in rare materials, especially lacquer. In the estimation of many sword connoisseurs, the great *tachi* blades of the Heian period and shortly after are the most elegant weapons ever made.

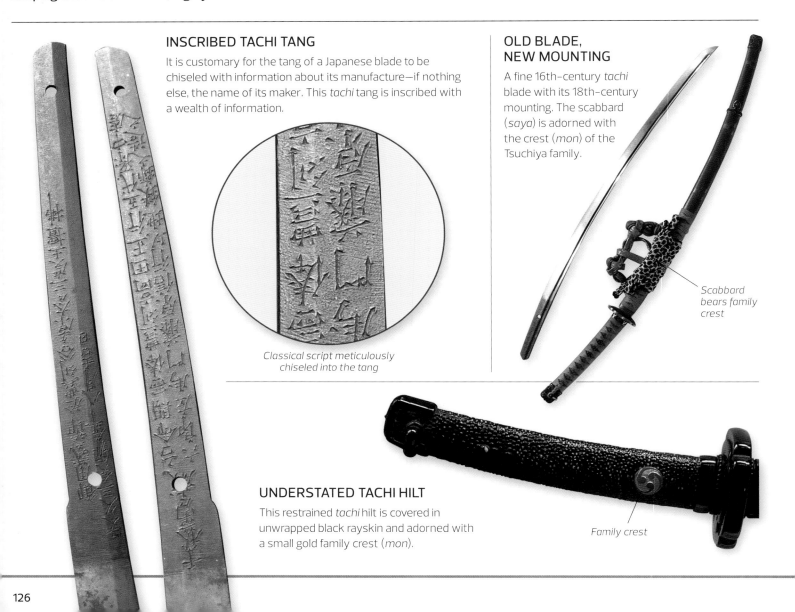

INSCRIBED TACHI TANG

It is customary for the tang of a Japanese blade to be chiseled with information about its manufacture—if nothing else, the name of its maker. This *tachi* tang is inscribed with a wealth of information.

Classical script meticulously chiseled into the tang

OLD BLADE, NEW MOUNTING

A fine 16th-century *tachi* blade with its 18th-century mounting. The scabbard (*saya*) is adorned with the crest (*mon*) of the Tsuchiya family.

Scabbard bears family crest

UNDERSTATED TACHI HILT

This restrained *tachi* hilt is covered in unwrapped black rayskin and adorned with a small gold family crest (*mon*).

Family crest

THE INFLUENCE OF HEIAN AESTHETICISM

Heian Japan was perhaps the single most aesthetically minded civilization in history. For approximately three centuries in which Japan remained largely free of outside influences, the Japanese nobility inhabited a hermetic world of poetry, art, music, and fine crafts, cultivating an appreciation of beauty that trumped all other considerations. *The Tale of Genji*, the world's first novel, was authored by Lady Murasaki while she served as a lady-in-waiting in the Heian court. It chronicles a world in which a courtier was judged more by his ability to compose a subtle and appropriate poem than by his skill at diplomacy or administration. Defense of the court was largely left to the minor nobility of the provinces, who rapidly gained power and formed a warrior class—the samurai (literally "those who serve")—that gradually took power from the increasingly isolated nobility of the capital, Kyoto. But even these warriors partook of the Heian cult of beauty; their swords and accoutrements were often decorated in urushi lacquer and gold (*maki-e*), and adorned with intricate and subtle techniques.

TACHI MOUNTING AND BLADE

A refined *tachi* blade and mounting. The blade dates from 1515, when it was forged by the great swordsmith Osefune Sukesada. The scabbard is covered in lacquer inlaid with mother-of-pearl.

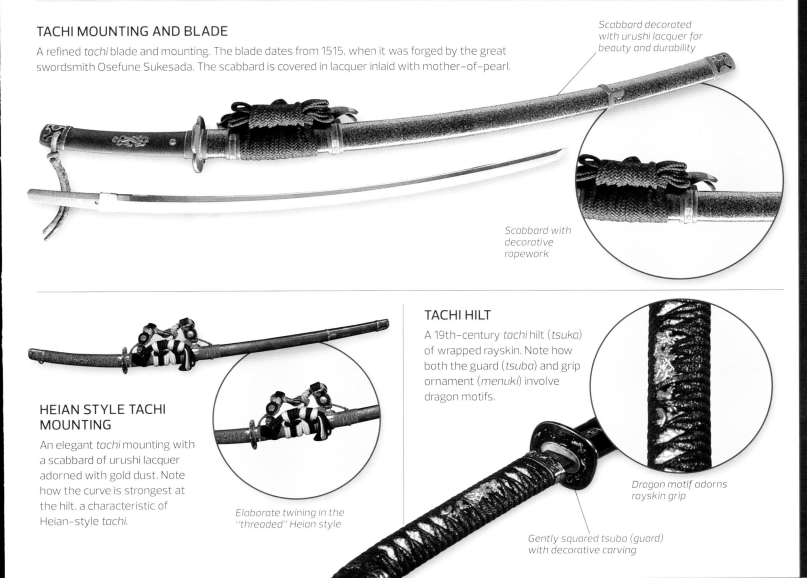

Scabbard decorated with urushi lacquer for beauty and durability

Scabbard with decorative ropework

HEIAN STYLE TACHI MOUNTING

An elegant *tachi* mounting with a scabbard of urushi lacquer adorned with gold dust. Note how the curve is strongest at the hilt, a characteristic of Heian-style *tachi*.

Elaborate twining in the "threaded" Heian style

TACHI HILT

A 19th-century *tachi* hilt (*tsuka*) of wrapped rayskin. Note how both the guard (*tsuba*) and grip ornament (*menuki*) involve dragon motifs.

Dragon motif adorns rayskin grip

Gently squared tsuba (guard) with decorative carving

The Tanto: Companion to the Tachi

Traditionally, the Japanese longsword was paired with a shorter, more utilitarian blade. In the Heian, Kamakura, and Muromachi periods—roughly from the 9th through 16th centuries—the usual companion blade to the *tachi* was the *tanto*, a short sword that, in some instances, was more of a long knife. Though warfare in the Heian period was governed by strict etiquette, it retained one tradition for which the *tanto* was an ideal tool: the Chinese custom of taking and counting enemy heads.

Both the *tachi* and the *tanto* were often endowed with elegant mountings, meant to showcase the taste and status of their owner. Similarly, *tanto* blades were, at least before the widespread warfare and resulting mass production of the 14th through 16th centuries, made with the same artistry as longer blades. Such aspects as their overall shapes, tip styles, and temper lines from differential hardening became points of aesthetic appreciation.

MASAMUNE TANTO BLADE

Archival images of a tanto blade by Masamune Goro (c. 1264–1343 CE), considered Japan's greatest bladesmith.

Exquisite temper line just above edge

TANTO WITH LACQUERED GRIP

An interesting *tanto* whose grip is wrapped in rayskin which has been smoothed, lacquered, and polished. The effect is very refined.

Straight but elegantly tipped blade

Polished rayskin grip

TOKUGAWA TANTO, BLADE AND MOUNTING

A refined *tanto* blade made by Kunimitsu Shintogo, teacher of Masamune. The later mounting, appropriately elegant in its lacquerwork, is decorated with the hollyhock seal (*mon*) of the Tokugawa family, Shoguns of Japan from 1600 until 1868.

Straight blade

Grip of rayskin (same)

Straight, restrained temper line (hamon)

SADAYOSHI TANTO

A famed *tanto* blade forged by the great swordsmith Sadayoshi in 1317. It has the straight temper line characteristic of blades by Sadayoshi's Hosho school of swordmaking. This blade is designated an important Cultural Property of Japan.

TANTO MOUNTING

An unusual *tanto* mounting with a Chinese-style guard and lacquered images of insects and plants around a lotus pond.

Scabbard with dragonfly and frog motifs

Plaited ropework

HONDA TADAKATSU: SAMURAI, RETAINER, GENERAL

Honda Tadakatsu (1548–1610), also known as Honda Heihachiro, one of the great retainer-generals of Tokugawa Ieyasu, founder of the Tokugawa Shogunate. He became known as one of Ieyasu's "Four Deva Kings." In over a hundred battles, Honda was never once wounded or defeated—he was known as "the warrior who overcame death itself"—and he had an impeccable reputation as a trustworthy retainer. Both Oda Nobunaga and Toyotomi Hideyoshi, the two other unifiers of Japan who briefly preceded Ieyasu, praised Honda as the paragon of loyal service and martial prowess. Though he was a fine swordsman, Honda was most famous for his prowess with the spear, or *yari*. His spear was named "Dragonfly Cutter," because it was said to be so sharp that a dragonfly was once sheared in two when it landed on the spearhead's edge. But Honda was not simply an old-school samurai; he also gained fame for his expert deployment of muskets as devastating weapons. In this portrait, Honda sits on a folding chair. He wears a *tachi*, paired with a *wakizashi*, a later and longer variety of short sword, rather than a *tanto*. In his right hand is a commander's baton. Hanging from his shoulder are Buddhist prayer beads, and on his head is his famous helmet adorned with simulated antlers. That suit of armor has itself become iconic.

Japanese Swords: Katana and Wakizashi

Most of the great blades of Japan—those designated National Treasures—are *tachi*. But during the Muromachi period (1337–1573), a new form of sword gained popularity: the *uchigatana*, or, as it later became known, the *katana*. The katana was not so much a new sword at first as a new way of wearing a sword: with the edge up rather than down, so that its wielder could draw it and strike an opponent in one rapid motion. Such was the nature of close combat at a time when samurai fought far more often on foot than on horseback. The resulting swords were also shorter, with blades seldom longer than thirty inches.

The *tachi* had been meant primarily for horseback—its edge-down blade allowed it to be pulled across the body and drawn without risking a cut to the neck of one's galloping horse—and its curve tended to be toward the hilt. The curves of katana blades vary, but they all tend toward the circumference of a circle whose center is the right shoulder of the sword's wielder. The katana is thus ideally curved for rapid slashing strikes, but can also be used for two-handed thrusts.

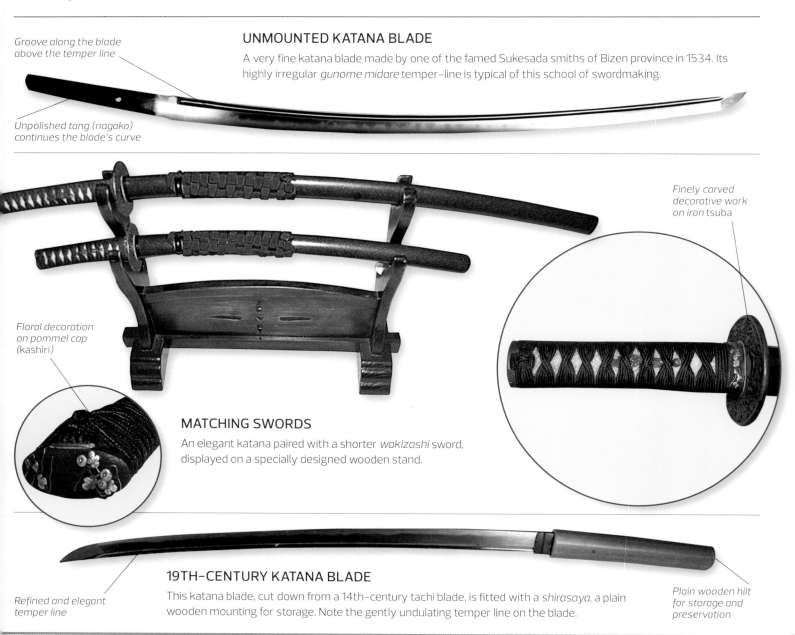

UNMOUNTED KATANA BLADE

A very fine katana blade made by one of the famed Sukesada smiths of Bizen province in 1534. Its highly irregular *gunome midare* temper-line is typical of this school of swordmaking.

Groove along the blade above the temper line

Unpolished tang (nagako) continues the blade's curve

Finely carved decorative work on iron tsuba

Floral decoration on pommel cap (kashiri)

MATCHING SWORDS

An elegant katana paired with a shorter *wakizashi* sword, displayed on a specially designed wooden stand.

19TH-CENTURY KATANA BLADE

This katana blade, cut down from a 14th-century tachi blade, is fitted with a *shirasaya*, a plain wooden mounting for storage. Note the gently undulating temper line on the blade.

Refined and elegant temper line

Plain wooden hilt for storage and preservation

DRAGON AND TIGER

Of the many tales of courage, honor, and rivalry among the swordsmen and the great *daimyo* (feudal lords) of Medieval Japan, one of the greatest is that of the remarkable rivalry between Takeda Shingen (1521–1573) and Uesugi Kenshin (1530–1578). During the middle to late years of the 16th century, the two men fought several battles, most of them inconclusive. Five times, the two men's armies fought at Kawanakajima. In the fifth battle, Kenshin fought his way through the melee until he reached Shingen, who was able to deflect Kenshin's sword blows with an iron war fan before his retainers drove Kenshin away. The moment is captured in a memorial statue at the site of the battle (right). The statue depicts Uesugi Kenshin weilding his sword on horseback while Takeda Shingen is depicted on foot in a dramatic defensive posture. But what became legendary was how Shingen, known as the "The Tiger of Kai," and Kenshin, called "The Dragon of Echigo," conducted themselves as rivals. They accorded each other the utmost respect, even exchanging gifts on occasion. Neither ever spoke ill of the other. Before his death, Shingen advised his son to seek the counsel and aid of Kenshin. When he heard of Shingen's death, Kenshin forbid his generals from taking advantage, and wept at having lost such a worthy adversary.

ORNATE IVORY MOUNTING

A close view of an elaborately carved ivory sword mounting from the Edo period (1603–1868). Though the craftsmanship is very fine, it is hardly typical; most fine Japanese sword mountings display a more restrained sensibility.

SIGNED TANG OF BLADE

The tang of a 14th-century sword. Since the maker's name was not evident, the blade was appraised by Honami Kokan of the famed Honami family of sword experts—hence the exquisitely brushed, not chiseled, attribution of the sword to the 14th-century smith Sadamune.

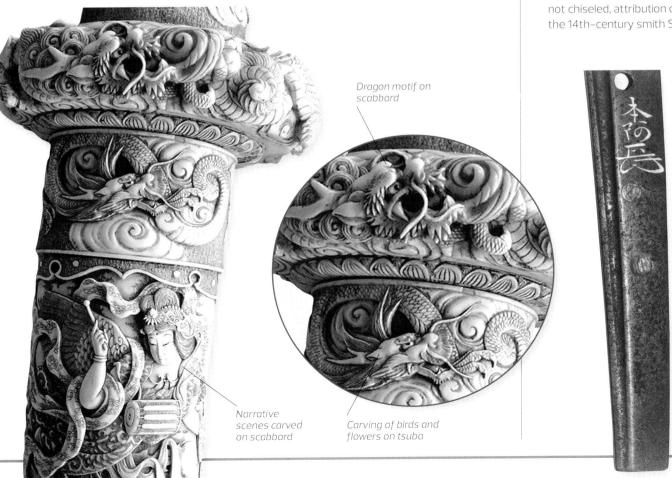

Dragon motif on scabbard

Narrative scenes carved on scabbard

Carving of birds and flowers on tsuba

Daisho

The katana gradually came to be paired with the *wakizashi*, or short sword, with a blade of up to two feet long. This pairing, known as *daisho*, or "big-little," became the iconic armament of the samurai. In truth, the use of the *wakizashi* remains uncertain; it is too long to be used as a knife. Some scholars have suggested that, in light of the custom of leaving one's long sword at the door when entering as a guest, the wakizashi was meant for indoor combat—but this would seem to contradict the principle of disarming oneself out of courtesy.

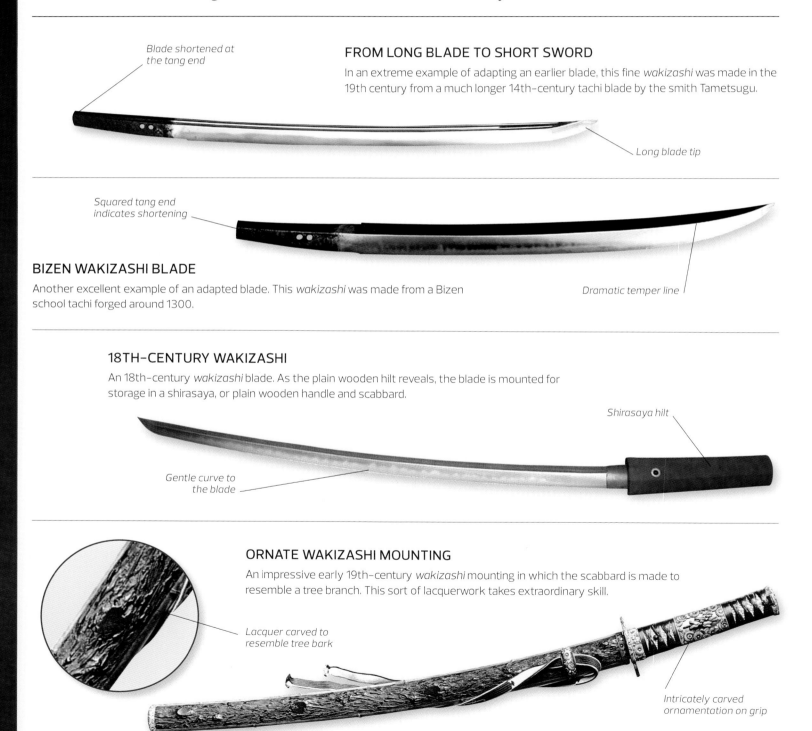

Blade shortened at the tang end

FROM LONG BLADE TO SHORT SWORD

In an extreme example of adapting an earlier blade, this fine *wakizashi* was made in the 19th century from a much longer 14th-century tachi blade by the smith Tametsugu.

Long blade tip

Squared tang end indicates shortening

BIZEN WAKIZASHI BLADE

Another excellent example of an adapted blade. This *wakizashi* was made from a Bizen school tachi forged around 1300.

Dramatic temper line

18TH-CENTURY WAKIZASHI

An 18th-century *wakizashi* blade. As the plain wooden hilt reveals, the blade is mounted for storage in a shirasaya, or plain wooden handle and scabbard.

Shirasaya hilt

Gentle curve to the blade

ORNATE WAKIZASHI MOUNTING

An impressive early 19th-century *wakizashi* mounting in which the scabbard is made to resemble a tree branch. This sort of lacquerwork takes extraordinary skill.

Lacquer carved to resemble tree bark

Intricately carved ornamentation on grip

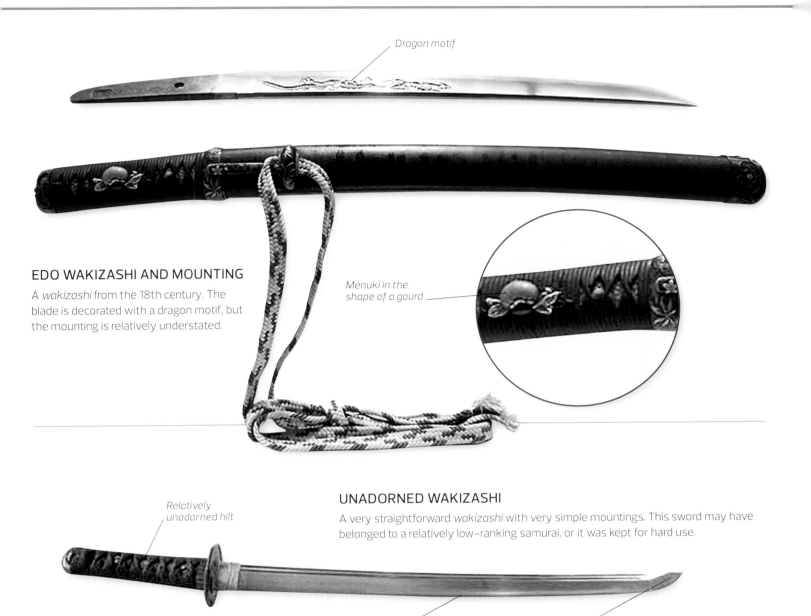

Dragon motif

EDO WAKIZASHI AND MOUNTING

A *wakizashi* from the 18th century. The blade is decorated with a dragon motif, but the mounting is relatively understated.

Menuki in the shape of a gourd

UNADORNED WAKIZASHI

A very straightforward *wakizashi* with very simple mountings. This sword may have belonged to a relatively low-ranking samurai, or it was kept for hard use.

Relatively unadorned hilt

Gentle curve to the blade

Long point design

MIYAMOTO MUSASHI: THE GREATEST SWORDSMAN IN HISTORY

Japan has a great legacy of swordsmen, but none is more revered than Miyamoto Musashi (c. 1580–1645). The son of a master swordsman, Musashi rose rapidly to prominence, winning his first duel at the age of thirteen. Over the course of his long career, he reportedly fought over sixty duels without a single defeat, once even battling and escaping an entire school of swordsmen when they ambushed him after he defeated their master. Musashi's most famous duel, however, was with Sasaki Kojiro, a feared swordsman whom Musashi defeated instantly—with a wooden sword. In fact, Musashi fought most of his duels with wooden swords. But he was much more than a swordsman: he was an artist, poet, and spiritual aspirant. The self-portrait at right, which shows Musashi holding both katana and *wakizashi* in a fighting style he called "Two Heavens," reveals how he exemplifies the ideal of *bunbu ichi*, or "the arts of war and the arts of peace are one." In 1643, he retired to a cave near Kumamoto, where he spent his time meditating and writing *A Book of Five Rings*, one of the world's greatest treatises on strategy and swordsmanship.

Anatomy of a Japanese Blade

The blade of a traditional Japanese sword is a work of art in itself. It is forged from steel purified through a series of repeated treatments. First, an inner core of relatively soft, low-carbon steel is formed through a series of laminations. That core is then enclosed in an outer shell of hard, high-carbon steel folded and refolded up to fifteen times. When the outer layer of high-carbon steel is wrapped around the softer steel, the arrangement produces a blade that combines hardness and resiliency. The edge is formed by a process of differential hardening, in which the smith coats the blade with heat-resistant clay, leaving the edge exposed. The border between the clay coating and the exposed outer steel forms the temper line (*hamon*) of the blade. Customarily, the smith will sign the blade, which will then be painstakingly polished by a different class of artisan.

MUNETSUGU LYONOJO TANG
An elegantly narrow tang (*nagako*) from a 17th-century katana. As was customary, the master bladesmith, Munetsugu Iyonojo, chiseled his signature in the unpolished steel.

Chiseled signature of swordsmith

Tang tapers to a narrow end

Subtle, undulating temper line

Point moderately long in proportion to blade width

MUNETSUGU LYONOJO TANG
The point (*kissaki*) of the Munetsugu Iyonojo katana. The temper line is subtle, in a gently undulating pattern known as *notareba*. The point is in the style known as *chū-kissaki*: moderately long in proportion to the width of the blade at its base.

(RIGHT) 14TH-CENTURY TANG
The tang of a tachi, probably from the 14th century. The swordsmith's name is clearly chiseled into the unpolished steel.

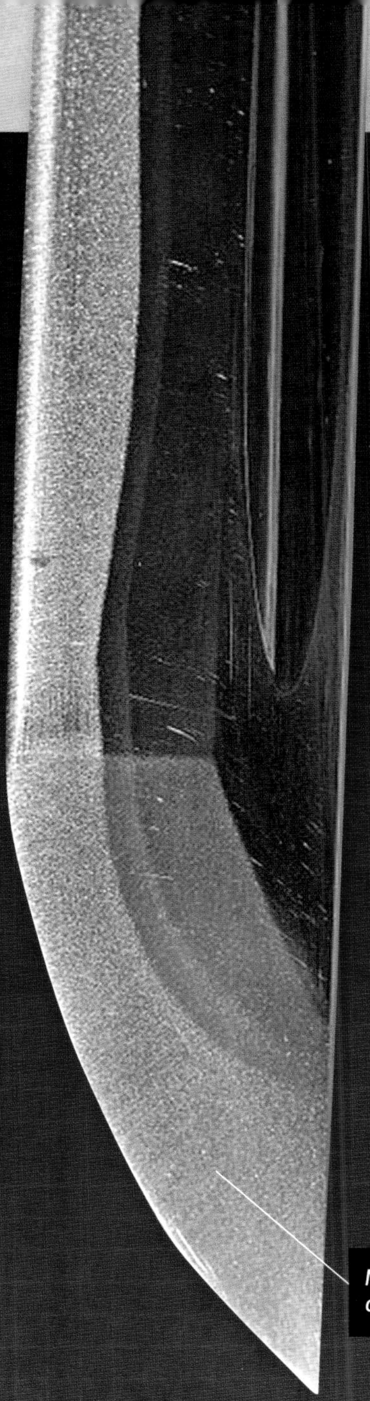

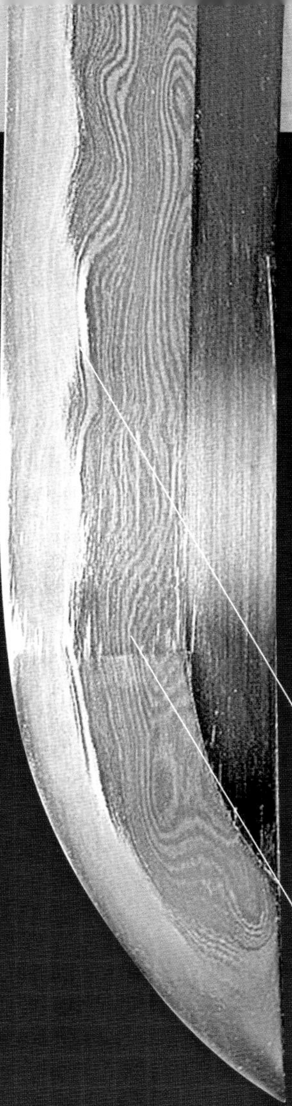

WOOD-GRAIN PATTERN
A view of a tachi blade's tip, showing the wood-grain, or *itame*, pattern in the steel above the temper line, which gently undulates in the notareba style.

Gently undulating temper line

Wood-grain pattern in the steel

TEMPER LINE
A detailed view of the tip of a katana. Note the straight, fine grain of the steel between the temper line and the spine of the blade, and how the *boshi*, the portion of the temper line within the point, ends with a shallow curve. The artistry and workmanship of the *boshi* are key factors in appraising a sword.

Straight grain of steel above the temper line

Irregular temper line

Copper-gilt sleeve (habaki) securing the blade to the hilt

Misty appearance of nioi

(ABOVE) TEMPERED STEEL BLADE TIP
The tempered edge (*ha*) of this blade is filled with *nioi*, a mist-like density of crystalline structures in the tempered steel.

(ABOVE) MIDARE-STYLE TEMPER LINE
Where this blade emerges from its hilt (*tsuka*), it reveals a dramatic temper line in an irregular, or *midare*, style.

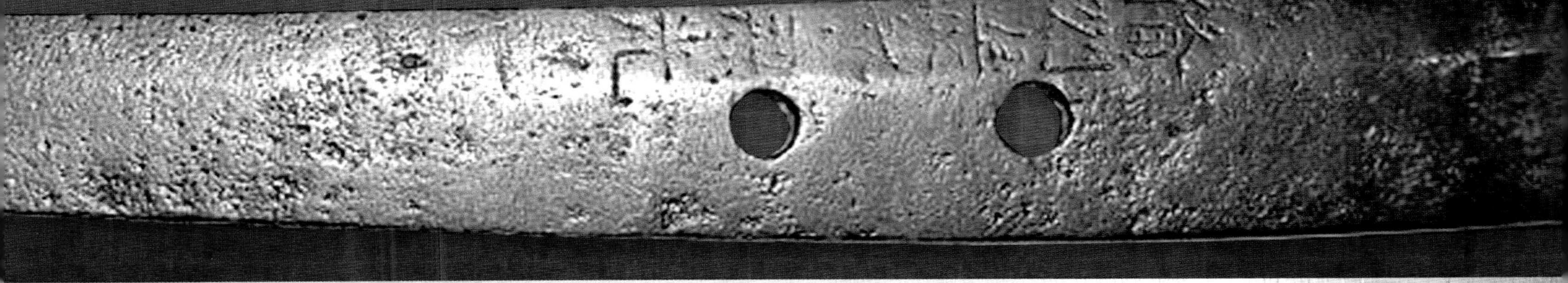

The Beauty of Japanese Sword Mountings

The Japanese reverence for the sword, combined with the country's rich artistic heritage, has led to a tradition of extraordinary blade mountings, or *koshirae*. From the Heian period to modern times, swords and knives have been fitted with hilts, scabbards, and accoutrements of intricate and distinctly Japanese design. In addition to carving, casting, and gilding, many Japanese sword mountings have durable and beautiful lacquer finishes.

Some of the most beautiful craftsmanship goes into the details of the hilt and scabbard. The grip (or *tsuka*), the guard (or *tsuba*), and the hilt-collar (or *fuchi*), which helps secure the guard), are all used as surfaces for beautiful and often witty decorative work. Artists frequently employ motifs and techniques to make matched sets of daisho.

Pommel cap
(*kashira*) *of a
monkey*

LIGHTHEARTED DECORATIVE TOUCHES

A hilt with witty motifs including one grip ornament (*menuki*) of a rabbit pounding millet, another of a playful fox, and a pommel cap (*kashira*) of a monkey. The grip itself is of ray skin (*same*) wrapped in silk cord.

TSUBA AND FUCHI

A close view of a Japanese sword hilt showing the guard and the iron hilt-collar, or *fuchi*, as they are mounted on the blade.

*Wisteria motif
on the scabbard
(saya)*

*Menuki of playing
puppies on grip*

*Gold dragonflies
on small* tsuba

ELEGANT TANTO MOUNTING

An exquisite 19th-century *tanto* mounting featuring motifs in lacquer and gold (*maki-e*) of wisteria, dragonflies, and puppies.

TSUBA WITH DRAGON IN CLOUDS

Two beautiful guards, or tsuba. Cranes and dragons are both traditional motifs in East Asian art.

Pommel cap with heron

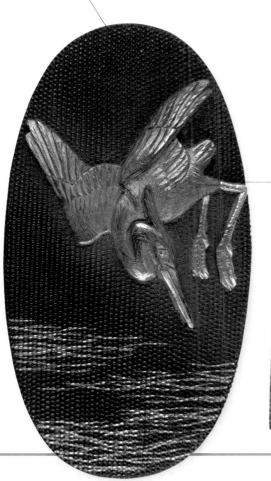

FUCHI WITH MAN FISHING

A witty hilt–collar showing a fisherman, his hat facing forward as he leans over to pull up a net.

THEMATIC DECORATION

A brilliantly executed matching pair of hilt collar (below) and pommel cap (left) in which herons are depicted against water signified by inlaid gold thread.

A Weapon Adorned with Art

The subtle detailing of Japanese sword mountings does not end with the tsuka, tsuba, and fuchi. Other components given decorative treatment include the cap, or *kashira*, on the pommel end of the grip; the handle of the small utility knife, or *kozuka*, tucked into the grip cords; and the end cap of the scabbard, or *kojiri*. The examples on these pages showcase the extraordinary craftsmanship that endows not only swords but also armor with remarkable beauty as well as functionality.

Tapering steel blade

Detail from pommel cap depicting traditional landscape scene

NATURAL AND SUPERNATURAL

Two very different pommel caps, one with a traditional landscape scene and the other in the form of a demon mask from *Nō* drama.

KOZUKA WITH GOLDEN HORSE

The handle of the *kozuka*, the small utility knife tucked into the mounting, is often finely decorated. This one depicts a gold horse under a cherry tree.

KOZUKA HANDLE WITH CARP MOTIF

This *kozuka* handle is artfully decorated with the image of a carp ascending a waterfall.

KOZUKA WITH CHINESE SAGE

A sage listens to the wind in the bamboo on this *kozuka* handle.

KOJIRI WITH BUKAN AND HIS TIGER

A scabbard end, or *kojiri*, depicting the Chinese immortal Bukan, who rode a pet tiger around his monastery.

Helmet with image
of Buddhist deity

LATE SAMURAI ARMOR

The aesthetic treatment of Japanese weapons extended to armor. Here is a full set of *tosei gusoku* armor of the Edo period, from the late 18th or early 19th century.

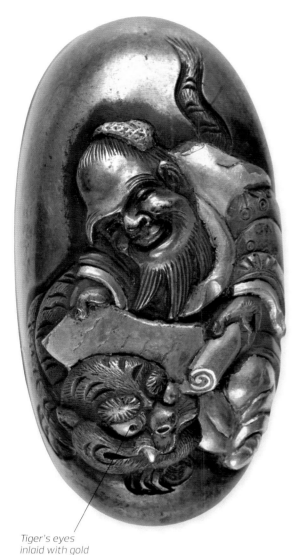

Tiger's eyes inlaid with gold

Decorated breastplate

THE CRAFT OF JAPANESE LACQUER

The art of working with *urushi* laquer is common throughout Asia; China, Korea, and South East Asian countries all boast long and accomplished traditions of lacquerwork. In Japan, the art often involves complex layering of colors and densities, inlays of abalone, and especially *maki-e*, or the use of gold dust or gold foil to create decorative pictures or patterns within the lacquer finish. The work is intricate and time-consuming. Raw *urushi* lacquer is mildly toxic, creating a painful rash on the skin, and it takes time to cure after application. Layers are built up gradually, and the finished work is subjected to a long process of polishing that, when desired, leaves a mirror-bright finish. The results are not only lustrous and beautiful, but also durable, which is why *urushi* lacquer is part of traditional samurai armor.

Japanese Pole Arms

Though the sword and bow were the most prized weapons of the samurai, and later the flintlock musket became a crucial part of Japanese warfare, pole arms hold an esteemed place in the Japanese armory. Samurai were often skilled in their use—especially when it came to the long-bladed spear (*yari*) and the curved-bladed pole arm (*naginata*).

Though particularly effective against mounted troops and much used in the wars of the 14th and 15th centuries, the

naginata later took on a more symbolic role, especially as the weapon with which samurai wives were expected to defend their homes when their husbands were away at war. The *yari* was central to the legendary exploits of the "Seven Spears of Shizugatake"—seven mounted bodyguards of Toyotomi Hideyoshi whose charge broke enemy ranks at a key moment in the Battle of Shizugatake in 1583.

SAMURAI YARI

A classic 16th-century *yari* with a stiff triangular blade with three sharp edges. It is mounted to a *shirasaya*, a plain wooden storage hilt and scabbard.

Stout triangular blade

Sword-like temper line

CLASSIC YARI

A classic *fukuro-yari* head with a short, double-edged blade and a sturdy diamond cross-section.

Pronounced central ridge in blade

THREE-BLADED YARI

A three-bladed, or *jumonji*, *yari*. This type of *yari* was especially effective against mounted samurai.

Long central stabbing blade

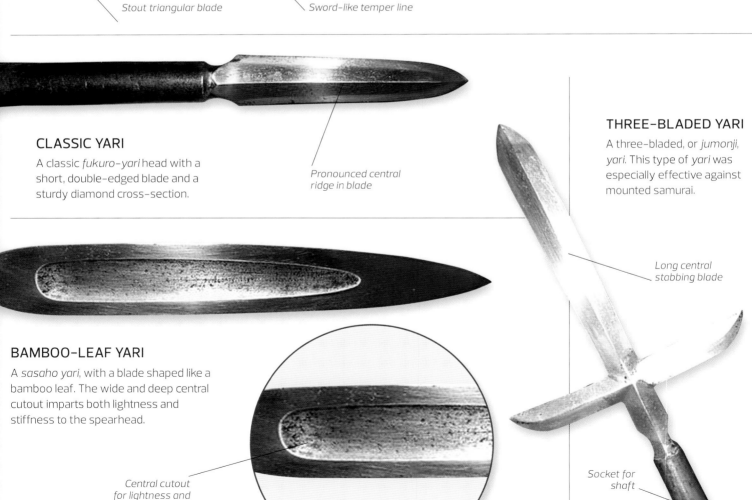

BAMBOO-LEAF YARI

A *sasaho yari*, with a blade shaped like a bamboo leaf. The wide and deep central cutout imparts both lightness and stiffness to the spearhead.

Central cutout for lightness and added stiffness

Socket for shaft

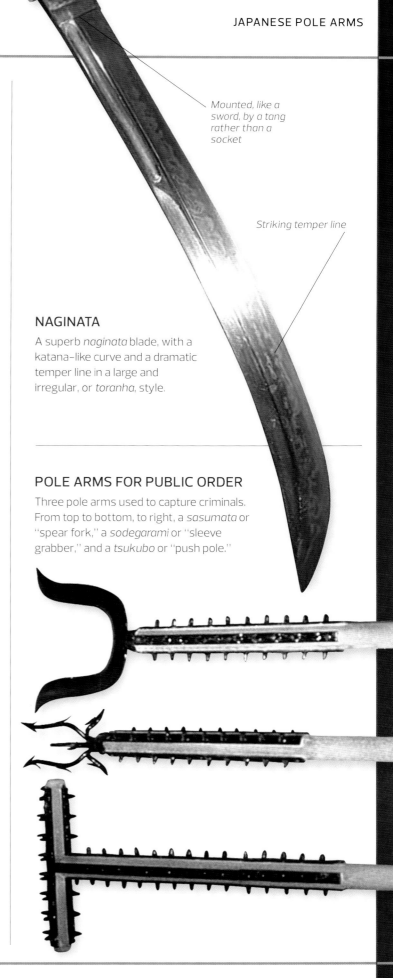

Mounted, like a sword, by a tang rather than a socket

Striking temper line

NAGINATA

A superb *naginata* blade, with a katana–like curve and a dramatic temper line in a large and irregular, or *toranha*, style.

POLE ARMS FOR PUBLIC ORDER

Three pole arms used to capture criminals. From top to bottom, to right, a *sasumata* or "spear fork," a *sodegarami* or "sleeve grabber," and a *tsukubo* or "push pole."

A POLE ARM FOR SAMURAI WIVES

A woodblock print from 1848 of Ishi–jo, wife of Oboshi Yoshio, one of the legendary 47 ronin who avenged the disgrace and death of their lord in 1703. Samurai wives were expected to be capable of wielding a *naginata* in defense of their homes.

A SWORD, EXTENDED

A *kikuchi yari*, a formidable weapon indeed. It is rather like a *tanto* mounted by its tang on the end of a staff. The quality of the blade is exceptional, and in the hands of a samurai it was quite deadly.

Single–edged, knife–like blade

Mounted by tang rather than socket

A Wider World of Weapons

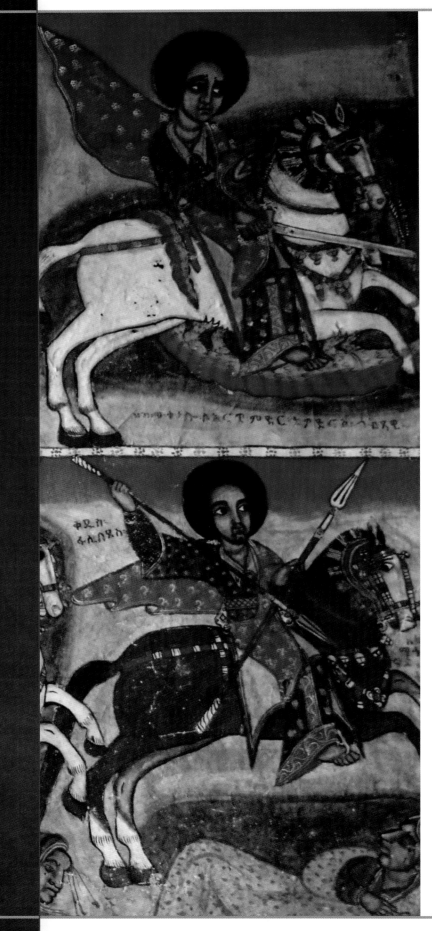

Ancient Warrior Traditions

Though the sword may have taken its most famous forms in the traditions presented elsewhere in this book, other cultures have their own long histories of weaponry. From the tribes of North America to the warrior cultures of South East Asia and the Pacific, a vast panoply of armaments is there for the exploring. Many of these weapons represent age-old warrior traditions.

AN ILLUSTRATION of mounted warriors from an Ethiopian church. Though their primary weapons are thrusting spears, one of the warriors also brandishes a sword.

Weapons of the Native Americans

The tribes of North America varied widely in their approaches to war. Some tended to avoid it, while others valued combat as the supreme test of character for both warrior and tribe. A few tribes of the Great Plains placed special value on close personal combat; "counting coup," or engaging in extraordinary acts of bravery—especially those that involved hand-to-hand contact with the enemy—was the utmost badge of honor. As the totemic images adorning them suggest, many of these weapons were considered charged with spiritual power.

PLAINS INDIAN WAR CLUB

A stripped-down and brutally effective war club of the Sioux. The length of the handle suggests that the club was meant for mounted as well as foot use.

CATLIN PAINTING OF CHIEF WITH TOMAHAWK

An 1832 portrait by George Catlin of Big Elk, an Omaha chief, with a pipe tomahawk. The two ends of the pipe tomahawk symbolized the choice of war or peace.

Totemic eagle head

HEAD OF HAIDA WAR CLUB

A formidable war club head of the Haida tribe. The figured head is made of antler—a naturally hard and durable material for such use.

Peace-pipe bowl on reverse of blade

NEZ PERCE TOMAHAWK AND HUDSON BAY CLOTH DROP

A Nez Perce tomahawk of classic design. The Hudson Bay cloth hanging from the end of the tomahawk was a staple of trade across northern North America.

Decorative feather

NEZ PERCE WAR CLUB

A classic Nez Perce war club with a head made of pipeclay, a kind of easily worked but durable quartzite.

Butt end carved as a human foot

A close view of the Delaware club, showing human features carved into the club's head.

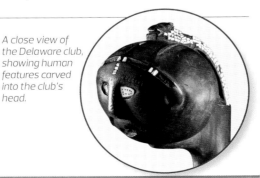

DELAWARE WAR CLUB

A 17th-century war club from the Delaware tribe, crafted in humanoid form from one piece of wood and decorated with beading and copper wire.

Anthropomorphic head

Weapons of the Indian Subcontinent

From Nepal and Tibet to Sri Lanka, the Indian subcontinent is home to some of the world's oldest and most developed civilizations. Their traditions of warfare and weaponry date back to well before the first millennium BCE. For thousands of years, rival kingdoms and civilizations have clashed across this vast region, and warrior castes have refined the construction and use of a wide range of weapons. Some weapons, in particular the sword and axe, have often been regarded as sacred objects and used either as symbols of spiritual discipline or ritual implements.

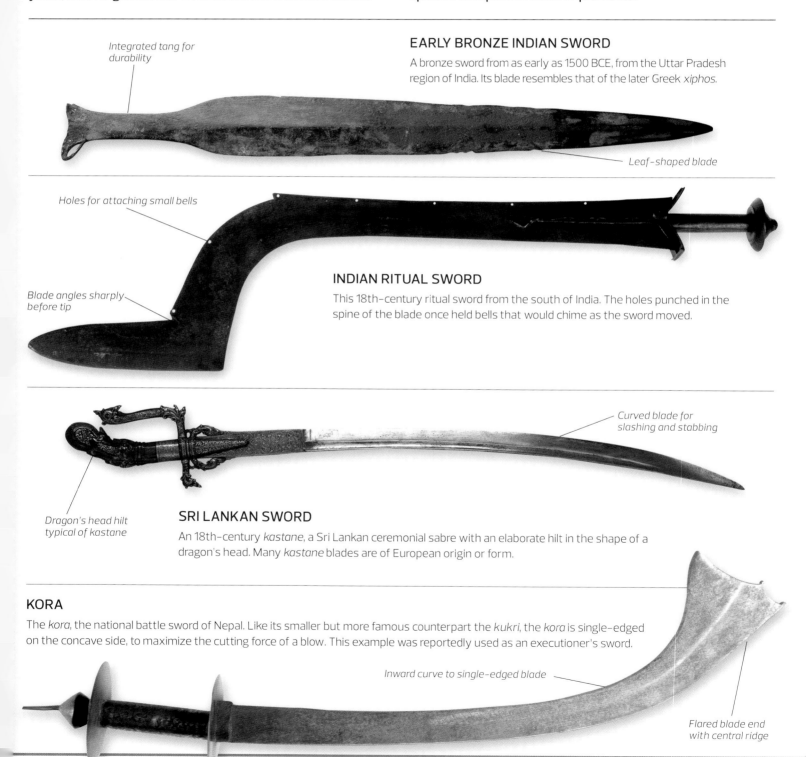

Integrated tang for durability

EARLY BRONZE INDIAN SWORD

A bronze sword from as early as 1500 BCE, from the Uttar Pradesh region of India. Its blade resembles that of the later Greek *xiphos*.

Leaf-shaped blade

Holes for attaching small bells

Blade angles sharply before tip

INDIAN RITUAL SWORD

This 18th-century ritual sword from the south of India. The holes punched in the spine of the blade once held bells that would chime as the sword moved.

Curved blade for slashing and stabbing

Dragon's head hilt typical of kastane

SRI LANKAN SWORD

An 18th-century *kastane*, a Sri Lankan ceremonial sabre with an elaborate hilt in the shape of a dragon's head. Many *kastane* blades are of European origin or form.

KORA

The *kora*, the national battle sword of Nepal. Like its smaller but more famous counterpart the *kukri*, the *kora* is single-edged on the concave side, to maximize the cutting force of a blow. This example was reportedly used as an executioner's sword.

Inward curve to single-edged blade

Flared blade end with central ridge

19TH-CENTURY TIBETAN RITUAL SWORD

A beautiful Tibetan ceremonial sword, with a carved jade hilt and a scabbard ornamented with Tibetan letters and a lotus image.

Scabbard inlaid with Tibetan letters

Ornate hilt with a sturdy knuckle guard

Two-edged hacking blade with no stabbing point

RAJPUT *KHANDA*

The *khanda*, a two-edged hacking and slashing sword used through much of India but particularly revered by the Rajputs.

TIBETAN SWORD

This richly mounted traditional Tibetan sword resembles the Chinese *jian*.

Silver hilt similar in form to that of a jian

Long, straight, two-edged blade

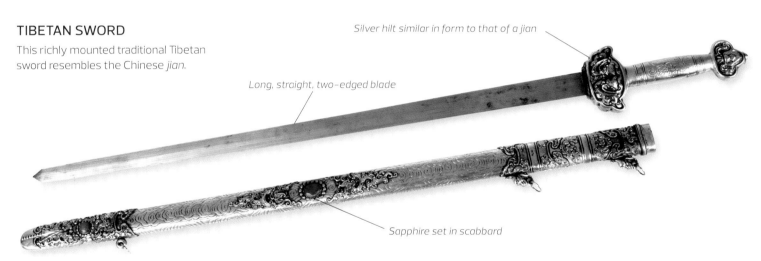

Sapphire set in scabbard

THE WARRIORS OF THE BHAGAVAD GĪTĀ

One of the great sacred texts of India is the *Bhagavad Gītā*, which recounts the spiritual crisis of Ārjuna, one of the warrior-princes of the Pandava family about to fight a pivotal battle against their rivals, the Kauravas. Perhaps no other book expresses so brilliantly the conflict between martial duty and personal conscience—and it resolves that conflict by viewing through the prism of Indic spirituality. Ārjuna, guided by his charioteer and teacher Krishna, overcomes his ignorance and attachment, and comes to understand the approaching battle as just one episode in the cosmic drama—a play in which none  of the individual participants is entirely real. Enlightened and liberated, Ārjuna rides forth into battle, secure in the knowledge that, despite war's destruction, death itself is an illusion, and he triumphs with a serene heart. Interestingly, a warrior on the opposing side, Bhishma, also fights with this higher awareness, and is allowed to choose the moment of his death. The image shown here illustrates the death of this great and saintly warrior. Though Bhishma has tried to prevent the war in which he fights, he is bound to fight on the wrong side. Free of all attachment, he performs his destined role and dies as he chooses on the battlefield.

The Gurkha Kukri

Sam Manekshaw (1914–2008), the renowned Indian Field Marshal, famously remarked, "If a man says he is not afraid of dying, he is either lying or a Gurkha." The Nepalese Gurkhas are among the most revered warriors on Earth. Their fearlessness and skill are legendary and their signature weapon is the *kukri*, a short sword with a single-edged blade angled sharply inward, ideal for hacking blows. Though heavy, *kukri* are exceptionally well-balanced and devastatingly effective.

The *kukri* is not only the signature weapon of the Gurkhas and of all Ghurka regiments in the British Military, it is also the national weapon of Nepal, a widely used tool, and an important ceremonial object. The smiths who make *kukri* are a distinct caste in Nepalise culture. Around the world the *kukri* remains one of the few truly iconic weapons, emblematic of courage and dedication.

HORN–HANDLED KUKRI
A presentation *kukri* with a handle made of horn. The presentation plaque on the scabbard reads "From the Officers 2nd Battalion 5th Gurkha Rifles."

NEPALESE PRESENTATION KUKRI
A beautiful presentation *kukri* from 1819. Its hilt is made of horn, its scabbard decorated with ornate metalwork.

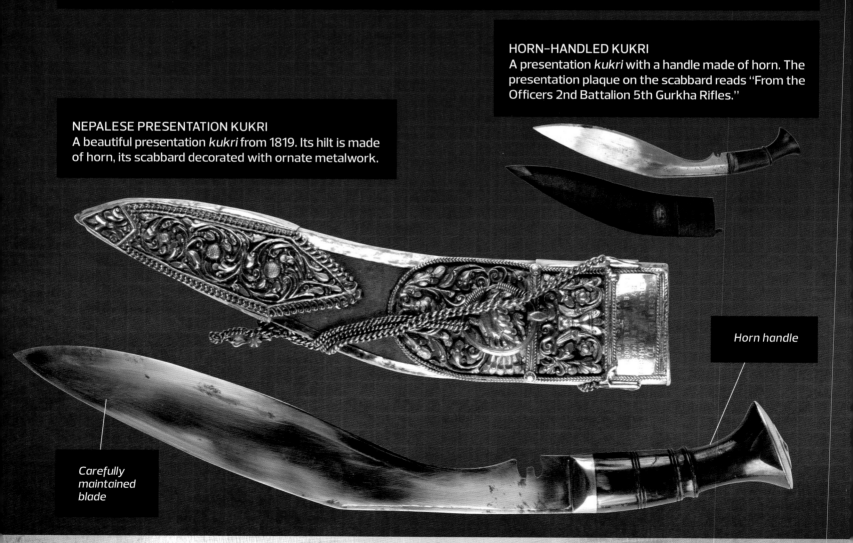

Horn handle

Carefully maintained blade

THE GURKHA KUKRI

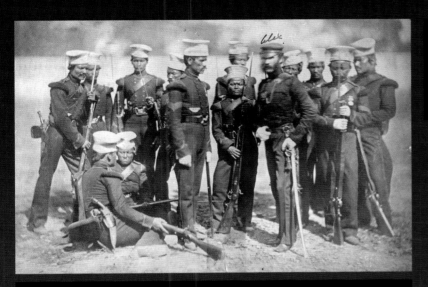

GURKHA TROOPS, 1857
The 1st Gurkha Rifles as they appeared in 1857. Note how the soldiers are equipped with large *kukri*.

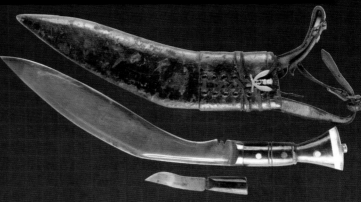

REGIMENTAL KUKRI
A 19th-century regimental kukri. The handle end is decorated with a regimental emblem, and the richly decorated leather sheath holds two small utility knives.

GURKHA KUKRI
A large kukri used in the First World War by a member of the 9th Gurkha Rifles. In the often savage hand-to-hand combat that sometimes accompanied trench warfare, *kukris* were ideal weapons.

Small sharpening knife

WORN KUKRI
A well-worn *kukri* with a carved horn handle. Many *kukri* are customarily used for utilitarian tasks such as clearing brush.

INDIAN-STYLE KUKRI
A late 18th-century *kukri* with a hilt in the pattern of an Indian *talwar* sword. The hilt is also inlaid with silver.

Sub-Saharan African Weapons

The many cultures and traditions of sub-Saharan Africa have produced a range of effective weapons, from spears and clubs to throwing blades of various kinds. African warfare, whether clashes of empires or local conflicts between tribal communities, developed distinctive tactics, some of which were used to striking effect against encroaching European empires.

MASAI SHORT SWORD

A *seme*, or "lion knife," of the Masai people of East Africa. The broad, two-edged blade is made purely for hacking and slashing attacks.

Traditional red grip

Two-edged slashing blade

Broad blade purely for hacking and slashing

KUBAN SWORD

The leaf-shaped blade of this sword, from the Kuba kingdom of central Africa, is clearly made for hacking. The Kingdom of Kuba, which still nominally exists, largely escaped the horrors of the trans-Atlantic slave trade and developed a diverse and rich culture.

Short grip with large pommel

Minimal hilt with no guard

MANDINKA SWORD

A fine sabre of the Mandinka people of West Africa. The shape of the elaborate leather scabbard resembles those found in the Sudan. Given that the Mandinka have cultural roots in Mali, this is no surprise.

Elaborately decorated sheath

Wire-wrapped grip

broad hacking blade

19TH-CENTURY NGBANDI SWORD

A two-edged sword of the Ngbandi people, who through much of their history were known as a warrior tribe. The broad blade, with its slightly inward-curved edges, is made for hacking and chopping.

19TH-CENTURY SWORD

A two-edged sword of the Yaka people of Central Africa. Note the substantial wooden pommel and the widening of the blade towards its point.

Hilt with secure grip but minimal guard

Broad slashing blade

YAKA SWORD

A formidable 19th-century sword of the Yaka people of Central Africa. Its elegantly shaped two-edged blade is attached to a hilt with a stabbing spike on the pommel.

Stabbing spike on pommel

Long, leaf-shaped blade

19TH-CENTURY POTO SWORD

A highly stylized blade features on this short sword of the Poto people of Central Africa.

Stylized, geometric blade

Chunky pommel

19TH-CENTURY NGBANDI SWORDI

This deadly sword of the Ngbandi people recalls a *kukri* in its angled, sickle-like shape. The double-edged end of the blade allows for a greater variety of attacks.

Kukri-like inwardly curved slashing blade

Two-edge portion of blade toward the tip

CEREMONIAL CLUB

An African club with an end in the shape of a cow or bull's head. Though the club could deliver a crushing blow with the snout of the head as the point of impact, it was most likely used for ceremonial or ritual purposes.

AFRICAN COPPER AXE

A fine African copper axe, with a stout shaft. Note the substantial heel of the shaft and the extra weight at the blade end, as well as the human face incised in the blade.

Human face incised in blade

NGALA EXECUTIONER'S SWORD

An executioner's sword from what is now the northeast region of Nigeria. Its stylized blade is clearly designed for cleaving blows struck in controlled circumstances.

Stylized hacking blade

Large, elaborate pommel

ZANDE EXECUTIONER'S SWORD

This executioner's sword has a long, sickle-like blade, single-edged except for the "false edge," or two-edged portion near the tip.

Sickle-like blade for sweeping cuts

One-handed grip

Two-edged tip of blade

SHAKA ZULU: WARRIOR-KING OF SOUTH AFRICA

Of all the African tribes, none has earned a greater reputation for martial prowess than the Zulu. Under the great king Shaka Zulu, their domain expanded, and they earned a tremendous reputation for their fighting prowess. Shaka, the illegitimate son of a chieftain, trained for many years and distinguished himself as a warrior while living with another tribe. With that tribe's help, he eventually took over the leadership of the Zulu.

Though ruthless in his methods, Shaka was also a skilled diplomat, and through a series of alliances and open conflicts gradually expanded his realm. He famously reorganized, rearmed, and drilled his warriors until they became unmatched as a fighting force. Their signature tactic was the use of two spears—one thrown to create initial damage and confusion, and a shorter one used for thrusting in close combat. Zulu warriors also became renowned for their extraordinary mobility and skill in maneuvering.

After being successfully treated by a British doctor after an assassination attempt, Shaka welcomed Europeans into Zulu territory—a decision that later led to armed conflict. Though he became familiar with European technologies and methods of war, Shaka held to his belief that Zulu culture was superior. In his rise to power and subsequent reign, Shaka made a number of enemies. In 1827, after the death of his mother, his behavior grew increasingly erratic and destructive, and his rivals—most prominently his half-brothers—found more support. In 1828 Shaka was assassinated.

ZULU SPEAR

A fine Zulu *umkhonto*, a spear similar to an *assegai* that can be used for both throwing and thrusting.

Curved, shearing blade

Central ridge in blade

NGBAKA EXECUTIONER'S SWORD

An executioner's sword of the Ngbaka people of Central Africa. Given its shape, it clearly is less than ideal for combat, but its tremendous shearing power served its purpose.

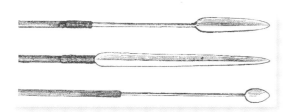

1908 ILLUSTRATION OF THREE TYPES OF ASSEGAI

A 1908 diagram illustrating three types of *assegai* in use by Zulu warriors. The Zulu spear had by that time become a legendary weapon.

PHOTO OF ZULU WARRIOR

This photo shows a Zulu warrior holding an *umkhonto we sizwe*, one of the short thrusting forms of *assegai* that were central to the successful campaigns of Shaka Zulu.

Southeast Asian and Pacific Weapons

The warrior traditions of Southeast Asia and the Pacific are, of course, as varied as the cultures that gave rise to them. Many Southeast Asian traditions show the influence of India and China, in both their weapons and their sense of the role of war and martial training as human activities. Many cultures of Oceania and the Pacific developed highly codified traditions of war, in which the honorable taking of heads was a measure of prowess and occasional cannibalism served ritual purposes. Such peoples as the Dayak of Borneo and the Maori of New Zealand have illustrious heritages of warrior culture.

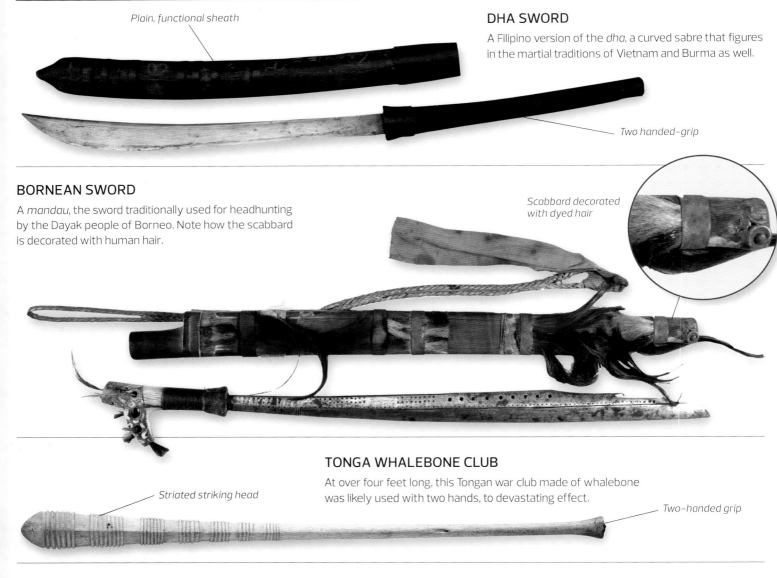

Plain, functional sheath

DHA SWORD

A Filipino version of the *dha*, a curved sabre that figures in the martial traditions of Vietnam and Burma as well.

Two handed-grip

BORNEAN SWORD

A *mandau*, the sword traditionally used for headhunting by the Dayak people of Borneo. Note how the scabbard is decorated with human hair.

Scabbard decorated with dyed hair

TONGA WHALEBONE CLUB

At over four feet long, this Tongan war club made of whalebone was likely used with two hands, to devastating effect.

Striated striking head

Two-handed grip

Polished jade, dense and strong

MAORI PATU

There is perhaps no more simple weapon than the war club, and the Maori *patu* is an archetypal example. This one, made of jade, would be enormously effective in the hands of a skilled warrior, who would tether the club to his wrist with a thong threaded through the hold in the handle.

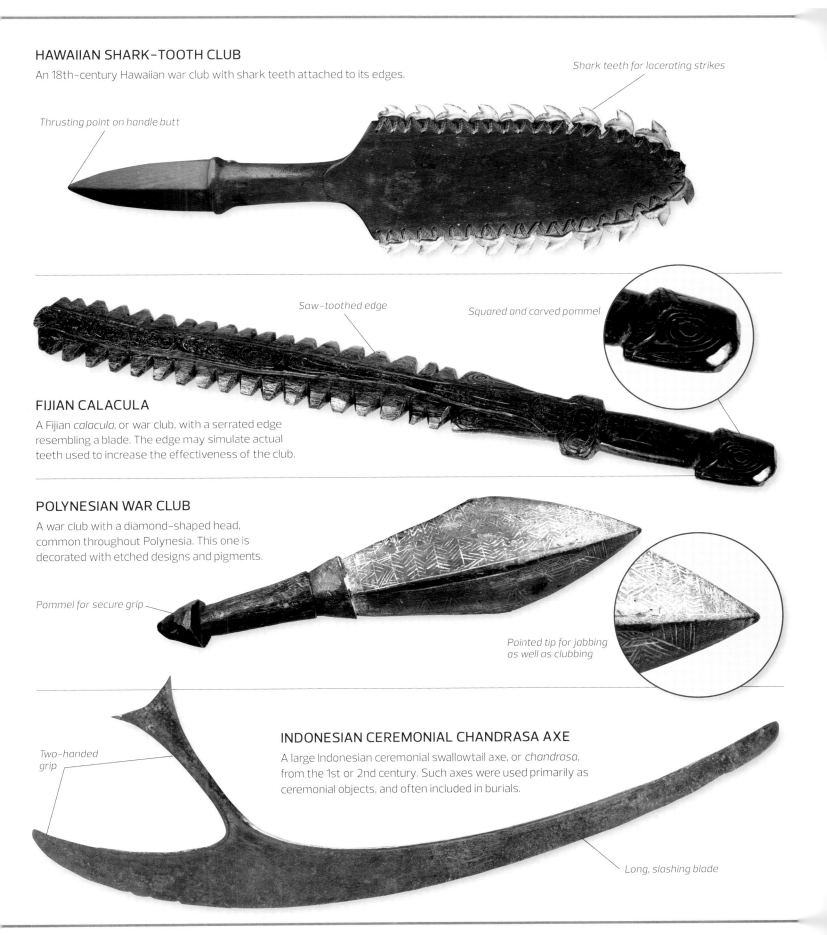

HAWAIIAN SHARK-TOOTH CLUB

An 18th-century Hawaiian war club with shark teeth attached to its edges.

Shark teeth for lacerating strikes

Thrusting point on handle butt

FIJIAN CALACULA

A Fijian *calacula*, or war club, with a serrated edge resembling a blade. The edge may simulate actual teeth used to increase the effectiveness of the club.

Saw-toothed edge

Squared and carved pommel

POLYNESIAN WAR CLUB

A war club with a diamond-shaped head, common throughout Polynesia. This one is decorated with etched designs and pigments.

Pommel for secure grip

Pointed tip for jabbing as well as clubbing

INDONESIAN CEREMONIAL CHANDRASA AXE

A large Indonesian ceremonial swallowtail axe, or *chandrasa*, from the 1st or 2nd century. Such axes were used primarily as ceremonial objects, and often included in burials.

Two-handed grip

Long, slashing blade

About the Berman Museum

Since the Berman Museum of World History opened its doors to the public in April of 1996, thousands of visitors have enjoyed its unique and varied collection of art, historical objects, and weapons. Located in the Appalachian foothills in Anniston, Alabama, and next door to the 75-year-old Anniston Museum of Natural History, which is affiliated with the Smithsonian, the Berman Museum's reputation and collection have grown exponentially since its inception. The Berman Museum's holdings number 8,500 objects and it has 3,000 items related to world history exhibited in its galleries. Among the many rare and fascinating objects from around the world, there are items such as an air rifle from Austria, military insignia from German and Italy, a scimitar from the Middle East, and graphically carved kris holders from Indonesia. The Museum attracts both a global and regional audience. All who visit can appreciate the historic significance of the collection and gain greater awareness and respect of other cultures.

Its five galleries—Deadly Beauty, American West, World War I, World War II, and Arts of Asia—exhibit items spanning a period of 3,500 years. A focal point of the Deadly Beauty gallery is the elaborate Royal Persian Scimitar, circa 1550, created for Abbas the Great, King of Persia. The American West gallery covers approximately 200 years (c. 1700–1900), emphasizing the United State's political, economic, social, and cultural structures, and their influences on settling the West.

The World War galleries use objects from the Museum collection to explore the causes and conditions of both wars, the historical significance of the countries involved, and the resulting political, economic, cultural, and social changes brought about by each war.

A rare piece of equipment in the World War I gallery is the Tanker's Splinter Goggles, used by tank personnel to protect their eyes and faces from metal splinters from machine-gun fire. Exhibited in the World War II gallery is the M1942 "Liberator" Pistol, as well as a large collection of Adolf Hitler's tea and coffee service, purported to have come from the last bunker that the Führer occupied. The Arts of Asia exhibit features an extensive and ever-growing collection of Asian textiles, ceramics, sculpture, jade, and metal.

The Berman Museum of World History is home to the vast and eclectic collection of Colonel Farley L. Berman and his wife, Germaine. Farley Berman, a lifelong resident of Anniston, Alabama, served in the European theater during World War II, and in the occupation force afterward. There he met Germaine, a French national. They were married and spent the next 50 years traveling the world acquiring historic weapons and artifacts, paintings, bronzes, and other works of art. Berman's self-trained collector's eye recognized the importance of items that were perhaps seen as ordinary, and he made it his mission to preserve a few. The Bermans established contacts—and a reputation—in numerous auction houses and among antique dealers in Europe and America.

The Bermans freely shared their collection with the public long before the City of Anniston constructed the Museum facility. Hundreds of military dignitaries and others were invited to their home for personal tours of their collection. Colonel Berman could best be described as a colorful storyteller and was notorious for firing blank rounds from his collection of spy weapons when guests least expected. He advised aspiring collectors to purchase good reference books, spend some years reading, and visit a range of museums before acquiring.

During the early 1990s, several large museums expressed interest in receiving the Bermans' collection. They were disappointed when Germaine proposed that the collection remain in Anniston. Colonel and Mrs. Berman's collection stands as the core of Berman Museum. Since the Museum's opening, many have recognized its importance and have contributed their own personal treasures to this impressive collection.

Glossary of Sword Terms

C

Center of percussion: the part of the blade where a strike produces little or no "buzz" down the length of the sword

Crossguard: the forward portion of the hilt that most clearly protects the wielder's hand

Cruciform: in the shape of a cross, as in many sword hilts if a sword is turned point-down

D

Damascus steel: a kind of steel originating in India that produced exceptionally fine, beautifully patterned blades—the term is often used now, inaccurately, for pattern-welded steel

Differential hardening: the process of forging and hardening a blade such that it combines a hard edge and outer "skin" with a softer, more resilient core

Distal taper: the change in thickness of a blade's cross-section from base to tip

F

Fuchi: the hilt collar, usually of cast iron, mounted behind the guard (tsuba) on a Japanese sword

Fuller: a groove along the length of a blade, meant to add stiffness while subtracting weight

G

Grip: the part of the sword actually held by the wielder

Guard: a catch-all term for the portion of the hilt that protects the wielder's hand

H

Hamon: the temper-line of a Japanese blade, formed during the process of differential hardening

Hardening: a precise process of heating and cooling that hardens a blade, particularly its edge

Hollow ground: a grinding process that creates a characteristic concave, beveled edge that is razor-sharp

K

Kashira: the butt cap on the end of the hilt of a Japanese sword

Knuckle guard: a part of the hilt that curves from the guard back toward the pommel to protect the hand

Kojiri: the cap on the end of the scabbard of a Japanese sword

Koshirae: a set of formal mountings for a Japanese blade

Kozuka: the handle of the small utility knife slotted into the scabbard of a Japanese sword

M

Mei: the inscription on the tang of a Japanese blade, often indicating its maker

Menuki: an ornament affixed to the grip of a Japanese sword, both as decoration and to improve grip

P

Pattern-welded steel: steel made by combining two different kinds of steel, which creates a Damascus-like pattern on the surface of a blade

Pommel: the butt end of a sword's hilt, which may serve to balance a sword

Profile taper:
the outline of the blade from its base to its point

Q

Quillon: another term for the crossguard, especially but not exclusively used in reference to rapier hilts

Quillon block: the portion of a rapier hilt from which the quillons and other bars extend

R

Ricasso: an unsharpened stretch of blade just above the guard, allowing a user to safely wrap his finger around the crossguard—often found on rapiers

S

Shirasaya: a simple wood hilt and scabbard for long-term storage of a Japanese blade

Shoe: the Western term for a protective cap on the end of a scabbard

T

Tang: the usually unsharpened portion of a blade to which the hilt is attached

Tempering: a heat treatment, done after initial hardening, to decrease the brittleness of a blade

Tsuba: the guard of a Japanese sword, usually of iron and often ornately decorated

Tsuka: the hilt of a Japanese blade

W

Watered steel: another term, now seldom used, for Damascus steel

Index

Acknowledgments

Moseley Road Inc would like to thank the following people for their assistance and patience in the making of this book: **The Berman Museum of World History**: Adam Cleveland, David Ford, Susan Doss, Evan Prescott, Sara Prescott, Quinton Turner and Kira Tidmore

Picture Credits

Unless otherwise noted, all silhouetted weaponry images are from the Berman Museum of World History, Anniston, Alabama, and photographed by *f*-stop fitzgerald and Jonathan Conklin Photography, Inc., with the exception of the following:

KEY : a above, b below, l left, r right, c center, t top

Cover l and c www.myarmoury.com 6bl br Los Angeles County Museum of Art 7l Michael Chidester 10cl BabelStone 10br Vincent Mourre/Inrap 11bl Sandstein 11br Rama 12b Hedning 13b Hiart 13tr Guillaume Blanchard 13c Walters Art Museum13tl Laténium 15tl Johnbod 15tr Laténium 15c Sandstein 15crb Dorieo 16–17, 18l Marie-Lan Nguyen 19bl Bibi Saint-Pol 19c Dorieo 19cr Xocolatl 19br Walters Art Museum 20bl Janmad 20tr Ticinese 21t Jastrow 21b Bibi Saint-Pol 22bl Anastasios71/Shutterstock 22br Marie-Lan Nguyen 22tr xlibber 23tr Marie-Lan Nguyen 23cl angellodeco/Shutterstock 23bl vaggelis vlahos 24tl, tr Jastrow 24bl Janmad 25 Marie-Lan Nguyen 26t Rama 26bl Jononmac46 27l Walters Art Museum 27r Ad Meskens 28–29, 30l British Library 31t BabelStone 31bc Schristian Bickel 31c Giorces 31bl Völkerwanderer 31br G.Garitan 32t, b Arild Nybø 32c Anagoria 33tl Silar 33tr Johnbod 34a Roger 34bl Arild Nybø 34br Keeshu 35br NTNU Vitenskapsmuseet 36 Anagoria 37t Torana 37c Anagoria 38c Anagoria 39tc The Man in Question 39tr Daderot 40t Incitatus 40bl S Marshall 41b Camocon 42t Rama 42b Walters Art Museum 43br Wolfgang Sauber 43t Martin Engelbrecht, Domschatzkammer Esse 44b Livrustkammaren 45r Nazanian 46bl, 47br Livrustkammaren 47t, 48t Walters Art Museum 48b Rama 49c Skoklosters slott 50–51, 52l OldakQuill 53c Walters Art Museum 53cb Rama 54c, bl, 55t, c, br Livrustkammaren 56t, c, b, 57t, c, b Livrustkammaren 58t, c, Livrustkammaren 58b Skoklosters slott 59b Los Angeles County Museum of Art 60t, c, b, 61t, b Livrustkammaren 62b, 63r Livrustkammaren 64t, b, 65t Livrustkammaren 66–67, 68l Livrustkammaren 69c, cb Walters Art Museum 70b Livrustkammaren 71c, cb, b Rama 72b Walters Art Museum 73cb Fordmadoxfraud 73br Ibagli 74t Walters Art Museum 74b, 75l Livrustkammaren 79t Rama 79c Livrustkammaren 80t, c, b, 81t, c Livrustkammaren 82t Ludo29 & Rama 82b, 83c Livrustkammaren 83b Ludo29 & Rama 84t, b 85l, r Livrustkammaren 85bl Thesupermat 86t, 87c, bl, br Livrustkammaren 88bl, br, tr Livrustkammaren 89ca Llewgriff 89b Rama 90b, 91b Livrustkammaren 92, 93t, c, cb Livrustkammaren 97t Walters Art Museum 97b Daderot 98 Livrustkammaren 99br Atif Gulzar 99 Livrustkammaren 100t, b Livrustkammaren 101t Walters Art Museum 101c Livrustkammaren 101b inazakira 103t Livrustkammaren 104–105 Livrustkammaren 106, 107b Livrustkammaren 108b, 109 Livrustkammaren 111t, 112t Livrustkammaren 113b Livrustkammaren 114, 115t, c Samuraiantiqueworld 116b Tropenmuseum 117bl Livrustkammaren 118–119 Walters Art Museum 120l Walters Art Museum 121t Los Angeles County Museum of Art 121bl Yutwong 121br Uploadalt 121c Editor at Large 121crb Hallwylska museet 122br Livrustkammaren 123c Joe Mabel 124cl Editor at Large 124cl, br Daderot 126bl Justin Smith 126cr Gabriel Rodriguez 126bl Ian Armstrong 127c Rama 127br Walters Art Museum 128cl Mitsui Memorial Museum, Mitsui Memorial Museum 128b Sano Art properties 129t Kakidai 129c Walters Art Museum 130t Walters Art Museum 130c Samuraiantiqueworld 130b Armémuseum 131t Qurren 131br Walters Art Museum 131bl Daderot 132t Walters Art Museum 132cb Rama 132b Walters Art Museum 133t Marie-Lan Nguyen 134t, b Marie-Lan Nguyen 135t, cb Parent Géry 136bl Samuraiantiqueworld 136r, 137tr, tl, t, br, bl Walters Art Museum 138–139 Walters Art Museum 140t Lx 121 140bl, cl, 141bl, tr Samuraiantiqueworld 142–143, 144l Bernard Gagnon 145cr Adam Jones, Ph.D. 145clb, crb Nez Perce 145b Skokloster slott 146t, cb, 147tl Los Angeles County Museum of Art 147tr Archit Patel 149br Livrustkammaren 149bc Sonett72 151t, ca, cb, b Brooklyn Museum 152cb, b, 153ca Brooklyn Museum 154tLorenz Lasco http://filhistory.com 154cb, 155t, b Los Angeles County Museum of Art